THE WORLD'S MERCHANT SHIPS

IMAGES AND IMPRESSIONS

Paintings by Robert Lloyd described by Roy Fenton

Victoria, the former *Kungsholm*, in the Solent (see page 92).

THE WORLD'S MERCHANT SHIPS

IMAGES AND IMPRESSIONS

Paintings by Robert Lloyd described by Roy Fenton drawing on the impressions of those who knew the ships

Ships in Focus Publications

Published in the UK in 2005 by Ships in Focus Publications, 18 Franklands, Longton, Preston PR4 5PD.

© Robert Lloyd, Roy Fenton, John Clarkson and Ships in Focus Publications
Paintings and sketches copyright Robert Lloyd
Photographs copyright John and Marion Clarkson and Ships in Focus.
Jacket design by Hugh Smallwood.

Printed by Amadeus Press Ltd., Cleckheaton.
ISBN 1 901703 67 3

CONTENTS

FOREWORD

Efthimios E. Mitropoulos Secretary-General, International Maritime Organization

It is not difficult, even for a layman, to see why ships and the seas have, for centuries, provided the inspiration for great art and, in particular, for great painting. To explore the contrasts between the apparent fragility of humankind and the great elemental forces of nature is a challenge worthy of any artist. Combine this with the sheer visual beauty and excitement of maritime iconography – sails and ropes, flags and banners, the ever-changing sky and of course the sea itself – and you have a panoply of artistic possibilities in which an infinite variety of shapes, colours and textures can be employed to speak of something altogether deeper and more elemental – something that touches the very essence of our relationship with the world we inhabit.

Shipping itself has been through any number of so-called 'Golden Ages'. There is no doubt, for example, that the early twentieth century's prestigious ocean liners or the magnificent square riggers of the age of sail could stir the hearts of all those that beheld them. Many would argue, and I would not disagree, that shipping today is in another truly Golden Age. Ships have never been more immense, never carried so much cargo, never been safer and more environmentally-friendly, never been so technically advanced and never been so sophisticated as they are today.

We all gaze in astonishment at the wonders of our brave new world – skyscrapers, bridges, dams, ship canals, tunnels and so on – stupendous achievements all. But there is no doubt in my mind that the marvels of engineering and technology that characterize modern shipping also deserve to be ranked alongside the very finest achievements of our global infrastructure. Mammoth container ships nudging the 10,000 TEU barrier yet still capable of 25-knot operating speeds; huge oil tankers and bulk carriers that carry vast quantities of fuel and other commodities around our planet economically, safely and cleanly; the complex and highly specialized workhorses of the offshore industry and the wonderful giants of the passenger ship world: even though they remain largely unsung, ships such as these incorporate the finest examples of naval architecture, marine engineering, design and technical skill.

Shipping today affects us all. From the economic perspective, we have now entered a new era of global interdependence from which there can be no turning back. No matter where you may be in the world, if you look around you it is almost certain that you will see something that either has been or will be transported by sea, whether in the form of raw materials, components or the finished article. We are all dependent on shipping: without it, one half of the world would freeze and the other half would starve.

We should celebrate excellence in shipping far more often than we do. I don't know how many people who see this book will have ever visited a modern ship but those who do should be prepared to have some of their preconceptions shattered. Ships today are modern, technologically advanced workplaces and the work of the International Maritime Organization (IMO) has played, and continues to play, a pivotal role in shaping that environment.

The direct output of IMO's regulatory work is a comprehensive body of international conventions, supported by literally hundreds of guidelines and recommendations that, between them, govern the safety, security and environmental aspects of just about every facet of the shipping industry – from the drawing board to the scrap yard. The result is an industry that is safer and cleaner than it has ever been before.

But has this somewhat sanitized shipping industry managed to retain its appeal for the artist? Does it still have the ability to inspire those who choose to paint and to move those of us who

view, admire and appreciate the artist's work? After all, thanks to the march of time and technology, the cutting edge of the elements, while never blunt, is certainly less keen than once it was; and surely a blocky steel hull and a fuel-efficient diesel engine lack the intrinsic romantic – almost organic – appeal of great wooden walls straining under an acre of sailcloth?

I think you only need to flick through the pages of this book to see that, in the hands of the right artist, the visual evocation of ships and the sea still calls out to something deep within us.

Robert Lloyd is a British artist who specializes in maritime subjects – indeed, a number of his paintings, depicting ships with which I have my own, personal, emotional associations, adorn the walls of my office and give me great pleasure and inspiration every working day. Two of them, depicting the *Corinthia*, on which my father spent eight years of total service, and *North Lord*, on which I was proud to serve in the early days of my career, are reproduced in this volume (see overleaf).

Indeed, every one of the ships faithfully copied here has its own story to tell: *Kong Haakon VII*, for example, was one of three oil tankers – giants by the standards of the time – which, in 1969, exploded within three weeks of each other, rocking the maritime world and acting as a catalyst for fundamental changes in tanker safety practices; the picture of the cruise ship *Canberra* at Gadani Beach awaiting the attention of the breakers not only shows the end of an era for a great shipping icon but also highlights an issue that is very current in the shipping world today, namely the conditions faced by workers in ship scrapping facilities; the almost unbelievable *Jahre Viking* – the largest ship ever built, sunk by missile fire during the Middle East war in 1986, later refloated, repaired and converted: fully laden, she could load a cargo worth (at today's oil prices of around the US$50 a barrel mark) more than US$210 million; and, of course, the marvellous sight of the *Queen Mary 2* together with the *Queen Elizabeth 2* at Southampton, emphasizing the resurgence in those majestic cruise liners.

If I may be forgiven for injecting a personal note once again, I had the good fortune to be present at the naming ceremony for the *Queen Mary 2* in January 2004, when the bow of the ship was unveiled by Her Majesty the Queen in a feast of sound and light which would have made even the Olympian Gods jealous. When, at the climax of the ceremony, the 'Ode to Joy' from Beethoven's Ninth Symphony was played, I remarked at the time what a happy combination this was of two of the great achievements of mankind. Beethoven's work has stood the test of time and, while no-one would expect the *Queen Mary 2* to be around in 180 years, I believe there is every possibility that she, too, will become a classic.

Through Robert Lloyd's superb paintings we can indeed celebrate many of the great classics of modern shipping and, I hope, recall the debt that we all owe to these workhorses of global commerce. But, more than that, we can revel in the sensory banquet that these pictures spread before us – the smell of the salt air, the gentle, reassuring throb of the engine, the sharp burn of an icy guard rail, the insistent cry of a gull somewhere above, the prospect of a distant shore. All of these and more lie ahead of us as we voyage through the wonderfully evocative pages of this veritable maritime masterpiece.

Corinthia at Marseilles

CORINTHIA
1939–1958
Hellenic Mediterranean Lines Co. Ltd., Piraeus

Hellenic Mediterranean Lines Co. Ltd. grew out of Hellenic Coast Lines Co. Ltd., itself an amalgamation in 1929 of some seven companies operating local services.

Depicted at Marseilles, *Corinthia* was Hellenic Mediterranean's first ship, bought in 1939, the year the company was formally incorporated. She was 28 years old, having been built for Koninklijke West-Indische Maildienst, Amsterdam as *Oranje Nassau*.

Corinthia was broken up at La Spezia in 1958.

Completed in 1911 by Koninklijke Maatschappij de Schelde, Vlissingen. 3,879 gross tons, 338 feet.
Machinery: triple expansion engines by Koninklijke Maatschappij de Schelde, Vlissingen.

North Lord off Japan

NORTH LORD

1959–1975

Priam Compania Naviera S.A., Panama (A.G. Pappadakis and Co. Ltd., London, managers)

A.G. Pappadakis began shipowning during the 1930s. Following the Second World War, a fleet of tankers and freighters from various European yards was built up under the Liberian flag. The ships were registered under one-ship companies such as Priam Compania Naviera S.A., specially set up in 1955 to own *North Lord*, seen here deeply-laden in Japanese waters.

For a modest tanker that was quickly overtaken in terms of size, *North Lord* gave satisfactory service. After 16 years' work she was laid up at Chalkis, Greece and did not trade again, being sold to Spanish shipbreakers in 1978.

Completed in 1959 by the Blythswood Shipbuilding Co. Ltd., Glasgow.
12,139 gross tons, 568 feet.
Machinery: Doxford-type six-cylinder oil engine by David Rowan and Co. Ltd., Glasgow.

OLIVEBANK

1962–1978

Bank Line Ltd. (Andrew Weir and Co. Ltd., managers), London

Bank Line is something of an oddity amongst British shipping companies, not least because it has survived when so many others have disappeared. Its story began exactly 120 years ago, when the 20-year old shipping clerk Andrew Weir bought an iron barque four years older than he was and renamed her *Willowbank*. Such was his success at managing her that within two years Andrew Weir was having new ships built. His fleet included the large four-masted steel barque *Olivebank* (1), which became famous between the wars as part of Gustav Erikson's fleet comprised of the world's last ocean-going sailing ships.

It was not long before Andrew Weir was ordering steamers, the first being the *Duneric* of 1896. As a relative latecomer to shipping, his company had to look beyond the well-established trade routes beginning in the UK, and Bank Line became established in many 'cross trades', so that its ships did not regularly visit British ports. They were also involved in tramp trades, which could see them in almost any major port around the world.

For services to the government during the First World War, Andrew Weir was made Baron Inverforth in 1919. He energetically returned to the shipping industry, and became an early operator of tankers and also joint founder of a liner company offering services between the UK and the newly independent Baltic republics, the United Baltic Corporation Ltd. In another bold move, in 1922 Bank Line Ltd. placed an order with Harland and Wolff Ltd. for 21 motor ships, the largest order yet placed by a shipowner for diesel vessels.

These vessels included the second, long-lived *Olivebank*, delivered in 1926. When Alan Burroughs joined her with a new Second Mate's ticket at Durban in October 1952, the twin-screw motor vessel's navigational aids consisted only of two compasses, two leads and a chronometer. As navigating officer, Alan's sextant usually provided the only noon position of the day. This, and especially navigating the ship at night inside Pemba Island off the East African coast, did much to enhance Alan's confidence in his navigation.

A voyage on the company's India-Natal Line was followed by dry docking at Calcutta. After several of *Olivebank's* plates had been renewed at the behest of a Lloyd's Register's surveyor, she loaded on the Indian-Chilean Line, the voyage concluding with a passage through the Patagonian channels. Unloading at ports on the west coast of South America, the long Pacific swells meant that it was desirable to use the 'insurance wire' for extra security. At open roadsteads the ship used both bower anchors in conjunction with mooring buoys.

Bagged sugar was loaded at Salaverry and Chicama for Philadelphia, from where *Olivebank* proceeded to Newport News to load pulverized coal for Japan. The voyage from Balboa to the Kobe pilot station took 38 days during which *Olivebank* saw only two ships and one glimpse of land, and was completed along a swept channel just a cable wide through a remaining Japanese minefield. Life in Bank Line was certainly varied.

After discharge, *Olivebank* was again dry docked: antifoulings of the time were ineffective beyond six months. Whilst proceeding from Kobe in ballast towards New Guinea, a typhoon provided the worst weather Alan ever experienced, and required the ship to steer 40 degrees off the intended heading. At Rabaul and Madang, copra was loaded for the Mersey where, in November 1953, the 27-year-old *Olivebank* was handed over to Mollers, her new owners. Alan, justifiably keen for a spot of leave after the 13-month voyage, declined the new owner's offer of taking the ship to Moller's shipyard at Blyth.

The third *Olivebank*, depicted in the main painting, was in many ways a descendant of the second vessel of this name. Following the Second World War, the woefully depleted Bank Line fleet began a measured programme of fleet replacement, which saw it take delivery of 55 ships over the next two decades. This *Olivebank* was sold in 1978, taking the new name *Golden Lagos*. She traded mainly in the Far East until early in 1984 she was sold to a shipbreaker at Kaohsiung.

Andrew Weir Shipping is still in business but, with much of its liner business having been sold, the emphasis is now on management, with six vessels for the Ministry of Defence. The owned fleet is much reduced and the remaining ships out on charter, so it is unlikely that the historic name *Olivebank* will be revived.

A travelled-stained *Olivebank* (2) of 1926 sails from Cape Town. *[F.W. Hawks collection]*

Olivebank (3)
Completed in 1962 by Harland and Wolff Ltd., Belfast.
6,461 gross tons, 483 feet.
Machinery: six-cylinder oil engine by Harland and Wolff Ltd., Belfast.

Olivebank of 1962 in the Panama Canal

BENVENUE

1948–1973

Ben Line Steamers Ltd., Glasgow

Two ports had the lion's share of British trade with the Far East: Liverpool and London. Liverpool was better placed for exporting goods manufactured in Lancashire, Yorkshire and the west Midlands. London was better placed for importing because of the large number of consumers within close reach. At Liverpool, the trade was dominated by Alfred Holt's Blue Funnel Line, who remained unchallenged thanks to local connections. At London, however, there was more competition, with Ben Line, Glen Line (who had gravitated to the port despite their Scottish origins) and P&O fighting it out with the likes of Nippon Yusen Kaisha and Hamburg-Amerika. So, whereas Blue Funnel could concentrate on providing frequent sailings from Liverpool with not very fast ships, at London the lines competed partly on speed. This became even more of a factor after Blue Funnel had acquired Glen Line in the 1930s.

Benvenue was part of Ben Line's immediate post-war building programme, and the drive to provide speed that had begun with her sister *Benmacdhui*, and continued with *Benclueuch*, *Benavon* and *Benalder*. Two sets of turbines were geared to a single screw to provide the 16 knots need to outpace the motor ships of Glen Line. A new colour scheme was adopted for post-war ships, with grey hulls and green boot-topping replacing the pre-war black and red.

Even more speed was coaxed out of the next class, the *Benreochs*, which began to enter service in 1952. The *Benlomond* of 1957, third of this class, is shown in the inset painting. Like *Benvenue* she was also from Connell's yard, and her Parson's turbines gave her a cruising speed of 18 knots. The ships of this class enabled Ben Line to offer direct sailings from London to Singapore, rapidly emerging as one of the Far East's major entrepôts, in just 21 days.

The Ben Line fleet included more than greyhounds: the company were also replacing their war losses with standard ships from British and US yards which were barely capable of 11 knots. And uniquely amongst companies serving the Far East, Ben were also building up a small fleet of dedicated heavy-lift ships, vessels built for the government during the war based on a Norwegian-owned prototype. Such a mixed fleet was possible because there was work not just for the fastest ships, work which enabled *Benvenue* and her four sisters to complete very respectable careers of up to 25 years, even when the quest for speed had seen them long displaced from the express services. *Benvenue* went straight from the Ben Line fleet to breakers at Kaohsiung in early 1973, the last of her class. *Benlomond* was also broken up at Kaohsioung, arriving straight from Ben Line service in October 1977.

Benvenue
Completed in 1948 by Charles Connell and Co. Ltd., Glasgow.
7,846 gross tons, 475 feet.
Machinery: two turbines by David Rowan and Co. Ltd., Glasgow, geared to a single shaft.

Benlomond off the Malaysian coast

Benvenue in the Thames. [B. Reeves]

Benvenue in the Bay of Biscay

OXFORDSHIRE

1957–1964
Bibby Line Ltd. (Bibby Brothers and Company, managers), Liverpool

Oxfordshire was the last of a famous, or perhaps infamous, group of ships, the purpose-built troop ships. In time of war, almost every passenger ship, from the most humble to the luxurious, is pressed into use as a troop carrier. This happened with Bibby's ships on at least three occasions during the twentieth century, beginning during the Boer War.

The company's ships were built for the trade to Burma via the Suez Canal and Red Sea, and in the days before air conditioning much attention was paid to optimising ventilation in the tropics. This was much appreciated during their trooping voyages during the First World War, and helped Bibby to win peacetime contracts for carrying troops to India and the eastern Mediterranean. These contracts initially used the ageing passenger ship *Derbyshire* of 1897, but in 1927 two cargo ships, *Dorsetshire* and *Somersetshire*, were converted into troop transports. Bibby was actually pleased to find a use for these ships, which had been built as ore carriers for a trade which never materialised. It says something about the low priority given to trooping that these ships were considered too slow for carrying general cargo but not for conveying soldiers. For Bibby, the trooping contracts were something of a lifesaver, especially as the interwar depression deepened, and in 1930 a third ship, the *Lancashire* of 1914, became a permanent trooper. The ultimate was a purpose-built trooper, and the *Devonshire* was such a ship, completed in 1939 just in time for another major conflict.

Oxfordshire was the largest and best equipped of the Bibby troopers. In 1952 the British government had asked Bibbys to have her built, but she was not completed until 1957, and by then trooping by sea had almost ended, as was related in the chapter on her near-sister, British India's *Nevasa* in 'The British Merchant Navy: Images and Experiences'. Commercial aircraft now had the capacity to move large numbers of personnel quickly, National Service was ending, and with the decline of its empire the UK was beginning to withdraw its forces from east of Suez. As a result, *Oxfordshire* spent only five years

trooping, although her contract with the government was for 20 years.

Bibby's disappointment at the ending of their trooping contract was mitigated by the compensation paid by the government for the early termination of *Oxfordshire's* charter. Bibby also found a new operator for her, the Italian Sitmar organisation, who wanted to take her on charter as an emigrant carrier. She was sent to Rotterdam to be converted for her new role at a cost of £2.3 million, probably more than she had cost to build. During conversion she was actually sold to Sitmar, mainly to get round the stipulation in the charter agreement that existing crewing arrangements were to continue, with British officers and Indian ratings. Conversion work was completed by Harland and Wolff at Southampton and in May 1964 the renamed *Fairstar* made her first voyage to Brisbane.

In her new role she was destined to be made redundant again. Emigrant carrying also succumbed to competition from airlines, and in 1973 *Fairstar* was converted into a cruise ship. Now began what was the longest phase of an extended career. Cruising mainly in the Far East, *Fairstar* was part of a successful operation that was acquired by P&O in 1988 to become P&O Sitmar Cruises. Ironically, P&O had been the parent company of British India, whose *Nevasa* – a contemporary of *Oxfordshire* – had been sent to the breakers in 1975.

After almost 25 years as a cruise ship, the former trooper was briefly renamed *Ripa* in 1997 and broken up at Alang, India later that year. *Oxfordshire* might have begun life as a fairly humble troop carrier, but the soundness of her hull and engines meant she was good enough for 40 years of demanding work.

Completed in 1957 by Fairfield Shipbuilding and Engineering Co. Ltd., Govan.
20,586 gross tons, 609 feet overall.
Machinery: four steam turbines by Fairfield Shipbuilding and Engineering Co. Ltd., Govan, double-reduction geared to two shafts.

Oxfordshire running trials in the Firth of Clyde. *[Ralston/Roy Fenton collection]*

Oxfordshire in trooping colours crossing the Bay of Biscay

GORGON

1933–1964
Ocean Steam Ship Co. Ltd. (Alfred Holt and Company), Liverpool

Gorgon was a cargo-passenger motor ship ordered for service between Singapore and Australia. This feeder service was a logical extension of Blue Funnel's service from Europe to the Far East, and was begun in 1891 with the first Gorgon. The local service continued after Blue Funnel extended their main routes from Europe to Australia in 1898.

When the second Gorgon joined the older Centaur, her ownership was shared equally between the West Australian Steam Navigation Co. Ltd. and Holt's Ocean Steam. However, the Australian partner soon withdrew having lost its only steamer, the elderly Minderoo, and fearing that a competitor would enter the trade. In a move which showed their confidence, Ocean not only purchased Gorgon outright but ordered a running mate, which was delivered in 1936 as Charon. The latter had an extra deck, which made her rather top heavy, and therefore uneasy in heavy cross seas. Both ships had been designed to use tidal ports in north west Australia, where they had to lie in mud berths at low water. Their specially strengthened bottoms, plus their excellent manoeuvrability, proved very useful assets during their war service.

When the Second World War came to the Far East in late 1941, both ships were in the thick of it. Early in 1942 Gorgon sailed from Melbourne to Singapore as part of a troop convoy. During the Japanese attacks on Singapore she was continuously bombed from 1st February, but was spared serious damage. On 11th February it became apparent to her master that the remainder of her cargo was not going to be discharged, and she sailed with 358 refugees on board. Heavily attacked by Japanese dive bombers on 12th February, the captain reported that only her extreme manoeuvrability saved Gorgon, but this almost certainly hid the skill and coolness with which he handled her.

Gorgon again survived bombing by Japanese aircraft whilst in Milne Bay, New Guinea on 4th April 1943. This attack was in response to the first Allied successes of the war against the Japanese army, when the Australians decisively halted the advance towards Port Moresby. Six of her crew were killed, and Gorgon was set on fire and so severely damaged that she had to be towed to Brisbane for repairs, but the ship's company had the satisfaction of reporting that two Japanese planes had been destroyed. Charon played an equally important part in supplying the base at Milne Bay, making around 30 voyages from Sydney in 1943 during which she escaped damage.

Post war, Gorgon and Charon resumed service, visiting many small ports in northern Australia. At Geraldton they would load flour, at Carnarvon the unusual combination of sheep and bananas, and at the pearling town of Broome boxes of pearl shell. Calls might be made at Port Samson, where blue asbestos mined in the Wittenoom Gorge was loaded. Cattle might be loaded at Derby.

Gorgon is remembered as a comfortable ship to sail on. She had a spacious music room and library in the forward end of her accommodation, and a bar and smoke room at the after end. Food was varied and interesting, served by immaculately turned out Chinese stewards. The crew were a mixture of Chinese cooks, stewards and engine room hands, plus Malay seamen and clerks. Their accommodation was segregated and each had their own cooking facilities.

During January and December, the ships' accommodation was altered, and as well as 100 or so passengers they carried 300 children from school in Australia to their parents in Malaysia. To accommodate these, bunks were fitted in the music room, smoke room and third class section aft.

Gorgon had a long career, but was hardly free of problems, especially in the engine room. When she broke down in Fremantle during 1951 it was found that her crankshaft was broken. There was nothing for it but to ship a new one out from Liverpool in Blue Funnel's Idomeneus. Installing the crankshaft in Gorgon meant cutting away the top of her engine room and borrowing the port authority's floating crane.

Gorgon and Charon were retired in 1963, replaced by the new Centaur. Gorgon was demolished at Hong Kong in 1964.

Sketch for the painting of Gorgon.

Completed in 1933 by Caledon Shipbuilding and Engineering Co. Ltd., Dundee.
3,533 gross tons, 320 feet.
Machinery: six-cylinder diesel engine by Akt Burmeister & Wain, Copenhagen.

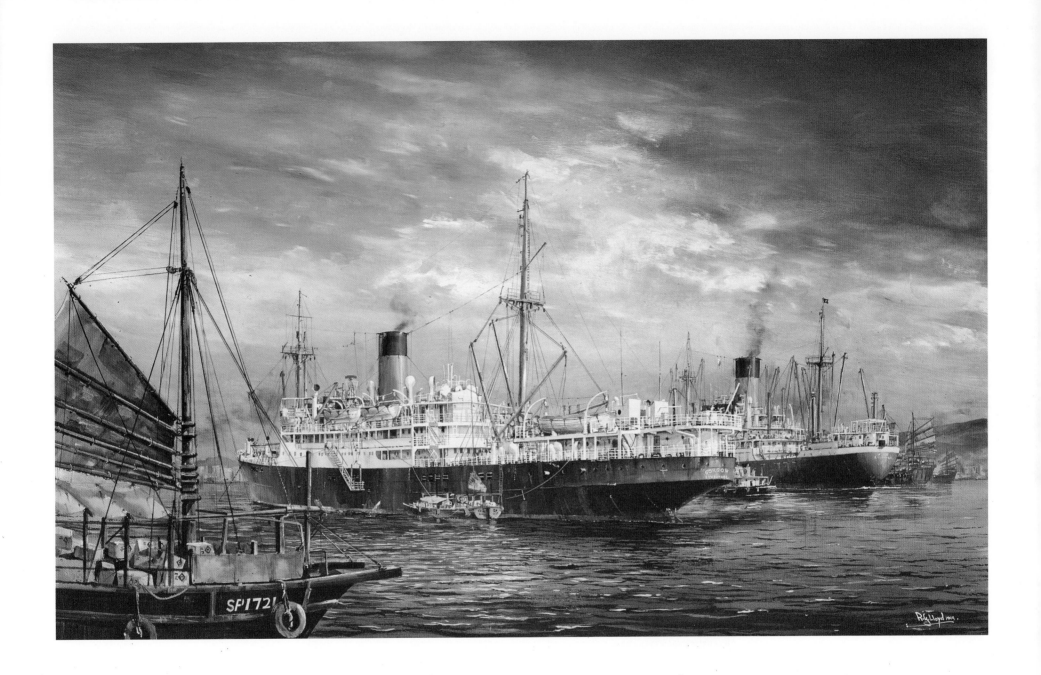

Gorgon in Singapore Roads

CENTAUR

1964–1985

Ocean Steam Ship Co. Ltd. (Alfred Holt and Company), Liverpool

As *Gorgon* approached her 30th birthday, Holts had to give thought to replacing her and *Charon* on the Singapore to Fremantle service. The problem of building one ship to replace two was handed to Marshall Meek, who had recently taken over as Blue Funnel's head of naval architecture from the legendary Harry Flett. Meek needed all his skill and enthusiasm to design a ship, the *Centaur*, that could cope with many different requirements.

The berths in the small, tidal harbours of north western Australia meant there was no question of building a ship twice as large as *Gorgon*. However, 190 passengers had to be accommodated. Then there was the refrigerated cargo; 5,000 sheep whose needs for space, feed and water were rigidly controlled; and – on southbound voyages – 700 cattle to be carried from Derby or Broome to Fremantle. A small problem amongst many was the need to ensure that this many cattle, who were almost wild, could be loaded during the limited time that the vessel's schedule permitted her in these harbours.

It was a challenge carrying so much livestock in close proximity to 180 passengers, many of whom would be regarding the passage as a cruise,. The solution was to install large fans in the livestock area, and to lead the effluent to the top of the two masts, which were made specially large for the purpose. Wind tunnel tests at the National Physical Laboratory at Teddington made sure it all worked. Unkind people said why bother, when the passengers would be mainly Australians!

The design problems were not helped by the Ministry of Transport in London, who became obsessive in their concerns over stability in the event of a collision. Marshall Meek remembers the Ministry demanding that a certain weight of animal fodder be sited in a certain area of the 'tween decks for a certain duration of the voyage. There was an implication that if the cattle were hungry and ate more than usual the ship might capsize.

Given size constraints, passenger cabins were relatively small, and to make maximum use of the space the beds folded back to make settees. On *Centaur's* first overnight trip from the shipyard at Clydebank to Liverpool, such was the novelty of a new passenger ship, that she was joined by many British and Australian journalists, who made full use of the Long Bar in the lounge. Late at night it was discovered that one of the Australian journalists had disappeared. After frantic searching by his colleagues, who feared the worst, a faint tapping was heard in his cabin. On throwing himself onto the bed, the Australian had failed to ensure that it was locked into position, and it had immediately tipped up and deposited him down the back of the settee, from where he had been unable to escape unaided. The bed-settee had to be broken up to release him.

Despite misgivings about whether such an expensive ship – she cost £2.5 million – was justified, *Centaur* proved immensely popular with regular passengers, some of whom came from as far away as Sydney each year to make the three-week round trip from Fremantle to Singapore. Marshall Meek was highly satisfied with her, and considered her successful operationally, aesthetically and financially.

Centaur was withdrawn from her service in 1981, her passenger accommodation no longer needed now that most travellers went by air. During the 1982 Falklands War she was chartered by the St Helena Shipping Co. Ltd. as a substitute for their requisitioned *St Helena*. Many regretted that she did not remain on this service, but in 1985 she was

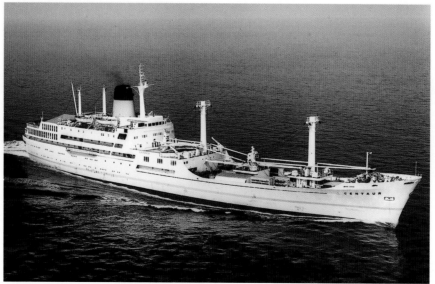

Centaur in the Malacca Strait. *[Airfoto]*

sold to China first as *Hai Long* and after 1986 as *Hai Da*. The trade along the southern coast of China, including Hong Kong, was perhaps one of the few remaining where a passenger cargo ship could still be usefully employed. Marshall Meek recalls seeing her familiar profile in Hong Kong, still running after 30 years, and wondering if over the latter years the Chinese had cared as much about stability as the over-zealous officials of the Ministry of Transport.

Completed in 1964 by John Brown and Co. (Clydebank) Ltd., Glasgow.
8,262 gross tons, 481 feet.
Machinery: two eleven-cylinder oil engines by Akt. Burmeister & Wain, Copenhagen driving twin shafts.

Centaur at Hong Kong

AUCKLAND STAR

1958–1978

Ocean Steam Ship Co. Ltd. (Alfred Holt and Company), Liverpool

This *Auckland Star* was the second of the name, the first being tragically short-lived. She was a development of the *Imperial Star* of 1934 which not only gave Blue Star Line a distinctive appearance, but also set superb standards in cargo liner design: big cargo carriers, with economical diesels and a comprehensive set of cargo gear. Launched at Belfast in June 1939, the first *Auckland Star* did not even complete a round trip such was the protracted nature of wartime voyages. On 28th July 1940 she was heading for Liverpool from Townsville with almost 11,000 tons of cargo which was of utmost value to the war effort - lead, steel, wheat, and refrigerated food - when she was torpedoed by Otto Kretschmer's *U 99* off Cape Clear, Ireland. Fortunately, there were no fatalities amongst her crew of 74.

Her successor from 1958 was no less distinguished. At 573 feet the second *Auckland Star* was Blue Star's biggest cargo carrier yet, an advance on her nearest sister, the motor ship *Wellington Star* of 1952. Like other Blue Star ships she was staunchly built and well maintained. As Captain A.W. Kinghorn has pointed out, they had to be. The weather round New Zealand can be horrendous, the South Pacific rarely lives up to its name for long and not for nothing has the North Atlantic been called the Cruel Sea.. Ships making these long voyages year after year, deep laden, driving along at 17 knots, had to be staunchly built and well maintained. There was little room for error. A single 'greeny' coming aboard could do untold damage. All machinery had to be constantly maintained at the highest efficiency.

And not only her machinery. *Auckland Star* had 26 cargo derricks with their wire runners and topping lifts, their manila and wire rope guys and preventers, their blocks, hooks and shackles, and their electrical winches - and all had to be maintained in perfect condition. To carry out this work the ship originally had a total complement of 74. In command was the master, usually a senior and highly experienced captain. Deck officers comprised the radio officer, four mates and two cadets. The chief engineer officer was responsible for all things mechanical and there were two seconds, two thirds, two fourths, numerous junior engineers, first and second refrigeration engineers, first and second electrical officers, a full crew of petty officers and ratings, a purser/chief steward

with his second and assistants, a bedroom steward, chief and second cooks, a baker and butcher, galley boys and pantry boys. Twelve passengers were comfortably accommodated. A doctor was not mandatory on a ship with less than one hundred souls onboard, but there was in those days no shortage of doctors wishing to take advantage of the free passage provided.

Captain Kinghorn's second voyage in *Auckland Star* took him behind the iron curtain, as she loaded frozen meat and butter for Bulgaria. There was an unexpected navigational difficulty in the Black Sea: the coast of Bulgaria was sown with mines. These were not old ones but new ones, aimed against the Turks with whom the Bulgarians quarrelled interminably. The approach channel was unbuoyed, but the harbour master gave clear instructions: 'If you head out on this course for two miles, and turn to port when this headland bears so much (he pencilled a figure in the chart's margin) you will be all right. That part is clear.' The day was clear, and the *Auckland Star* safely navigated the minefield.

But at Varna there was another problem: its food shops resembled Old Mother Hubbard's cupboard. The *Auckland Star's* crew now numbered 68, and it was impossible to find enough fruit and vegetables for them, although it was summer. Bad weather and the demands of Russia were blamed for the shortage. The purser bought what he could in so-called Free Market where, contrary to the ideology of socialism, farmers were allowed to sell their own produce.

Approaching her 20th birthday in 1978, *Auckland Star* was sold to breakers in Pakistan. She was too old for conversion to a container ship and, as a turbine ship, few if any flag-of-convenience operators were interested in her. Demolition began on Gadani Beach in August 1978. A third *Auckland Star* was built in 1985, but we are unlikely to see another: Blue Star disposed of its container operations to P&O and left shipping in 2001 with its reefers sold to Norway.

Completed in 1958 by Cammell Laird and Co. (Shipbuilders and Engineers) Ltd., Birkenhead. 11,799 gross tons, 573 feet. Machinery: two steam turbines by Cammell Laird and Co. (Shipbuilders and Engineers) Ltd., Birkenhead, geared to one shaft.

Auckland Star in the Mersey. [J. & M. Clarkson]

Auckland Star at sea

BRASILIA STAR

1957–1979

Ocean Steam Ship Co. Ltd. (Alfred Holt and Company), Liverpool

Blue Star Line achieved something of a reputation for changing their ships' names with what seemed almost dizzying frequence. Their main liner routes ranged from the UK/Europe to North and South America, South and East Africa, Australia, New Zealand, Middle and Far East and the Pacific Islands, with a few places in between. To serve these trades they had a pool of around forty versatile vessels - fine ships, mostly able to carry refrigerated cargo as well as general. To keep pace with various requirements a ship would be taken up from one trade and placed on another, with appropriate name change if deemed desirable.

Queensland Star was one of a rather classy series built in the late 1950s for the proposed chilled beef trade between Queensland and the UK. When Queensland chilled beef did not come up to expectations - due to uncooperative Australian weather over several seasons - the ship was placed in other trades, at first retaining her original name. But when Blue Star Line's prestigious 25-year-old regular cargo passenger liners were withdrawn from the United Kingdom to east coast of South American service, *Queensland Star*, at the time unloading Tasmanian apples in Cardiff on 9th June 1972, was renamed *Brasilia Star*.

Captain A.W. Kinghorn was standing by as master at the time. Late one afternoon the Harbour Master came aboard, telling him to shift the ship along the quay that evening to allow room for an expected arrival. Berthed on the outer harbour wall she had no engines at that short notice, the chief engineer having a big survey job on. On board were a few Chinese sailors, an excellent Scottish chief officer and one cadet; a bare minimum required for this kind of warping manoeuvre. The most important thing in this evolution with an offshore wind is to ensure never to let all the ropes go at the same time - otherwise the ship will drift across the dock. The master would be on the bridge controlling the manoeuvre by walkie-talkie. The chief officer forward knew exactly what to do: pass the lines ahead one at a time to the men onshore - use ship's windlass and winches to heave her ahead - have both anchors ready to let go should all ropes be accidentally let go at once. The cadet, who had never done this before, would be in charge of

handling the ropes to the quay aft, so he was shown what to do using ship models. Despite an increasingly gusty offshore wind and thanks to the chief officer's and cadet's perspicacity, *Brasilia Star* shifted along the quay without mishap.

In Santos, on her return voyage, *Brasilia Star* loaded frozen lamb and cartons of tinned coffee. It was here that the chief officer decided he had a much-needed chance to paint right round the ship's grey hull. Unfortunately the Chinese crew had proved themselves temperamentally and physically unsuitable for this hardworking South American service. One night at sea Captain Kinghorn was called down to the crew accommodation to quell a knife fight between recalcitrant seamen. His sudden appearance in full uniform gave them pause for thought and two knives were meekly handed over - but how could fellows like that be trusted? They had, perhaps, been spoiled on their previous long, leisurely Australian voyages where unworked overtime payment was generous. But here they had to work hard tending cargo gear, shifting hatch beams and heavy, old-fashioned insulated hatch plugs at every deck in every port as rapid loading proceeded. And when the chief officer gave them this painting job they replied 'No can do!' (not, they demanded, without at least double overtime pay plus a bonus). 'O.K.' said the chief officer calmly, 'No more overtime for you lot,' and he and the two cadets proceeded to paint round the entire ship in two days. As the sailors depended on their overtime payments for spending money they lost face with their engine room and catering shipmates - and more importantly, lost cash - and pleaded to be allowed to resume work. But the officers were adamant, and at the end of the voyage the crew was replaced.

The ship's name fluctuated between *Queensland Star* and *Brasilia Star* until 1979 when - superseded by container shipping - she went to Kaohsiung breakers at the early age of 22.

Brasilia Star. [J.K. Byass]

Completed in 1957 by Fairfield Shipbuilding and Engineering Co. Ltd., Govan.
10,657 gross tons, 512 feet.
Machinery: Doxford-type five-cylinder oil engine by Fairfield Shipbuilding and Engineering Co. Ltd., Govan.

Brasilia Star in the Solent

MARGARET BOWATER

1955–1968

Bowaters Steamship Co. Ltd., London

The Bowater Steamship Co. Ltd. was the creation of Britain's biggest paper company, at the time it had reached the zenith of its power. It was also an expression of the dynamism and pride of one man, Sir Eric Bowater. Eric Bowater was 'a businessman of exceptional force, daring and creativeness'. By building and buying paper mills, he transformed the agency business he had inherited from his grandfather into the UK's leading paper manufacturer. His mills usually had good access by water, like that alongside the Manchester Ship Canal at Ellesmere Port in Cheshire which was built to supply newsprint for Manchester editions of daily papers.

Bowaters' shipping interests began in 1938 when two steamers were acquired along with a pulp and paper mill at Corner Brook in Newfoundland. Major expansion came after the Second World War, with the formation of the Bowaters Steamship Co. Ltd. *Margaret Bowater* was its first ship and with her sister, *Sarah Bowater,* was designed primarily to carry newsprint on the Atlantic coast of North America from Corner Brook down to the Gulf of Mexico and across the Atlantic to the United Kingdom. A newsprint roll is large and heavy, but also very vulnerable to damage: a one-inch tear in a roll could make a mile of paper unusable. To avoid such expensive damage pillars were eliminated from the holds of *Margaret Bowater* and her sisters, and wherever possible other obstructions were avoided. Sparring in the holds was covered with rubber to help prevent it damaging the paper rolls.

Although only a modest newsprint carrier, *Margaret Bowater* was built and run more like a high-class cargo liner. Named after Sir Eric Bowater's wife, she had excellent accommodation for crew and a few passengers. Turbines drove her along smoothly, if uneconomically, at 14 knots.

Management of Bowaters' ships by Cayzer, Irvine (and later the British and Commonwealth Group) meant that Clan Line officers were regularly seconded to the ships. The contrasts between the heat of Calcutta, the ambience of Cape Town and the ice of Corner Brook could hardly be greater. In 1966 and 1967 Captain Tony Blackler enjoyed several of these contrasts, and records how successive tours of duty might be made in *Margaret Bowater* from the Baltic to British

paper mills and from Corner Brook to the southern USA; in *Edinburgh Castle* to Cape Town; and in *Clan Menzies* to the Indian Ocean.

From September 1966 Tony was second mate in *Margaret Bowater* and he records how she first shuttled between Holmsund in Sweden and Northfleet or Ellesmere Port with pulp, voyages taking only five or six days. After drydocking at North Shields in December 1966, voyage 204 took her to Corner Brook, where the January ice was two feet thick. From here newsprint was taken down the US east coast to Savannah, Norfolk and Richmond. Reaching the last-named meant sailing up the James River, and it was found that flying the Confederate flag as a courtesy ensign went down particularly well with the locals. Subsequent voyages were made from Corner Brook to Baltimore and New York. The ship was late arriving at New York, having slowed for fog, but the agent was insistent that 'Fog is no excuse for being late here.' The master retorted that it certainly was, and was backed up by the company even though they had to pay the dockers stand-by time.

Ice was a hazard even comparatively late in the year. In March 1967 *Margaret Bowater* was stuck in the ice off Cape Ray, Newfoundland and called for assistance. A small Canadian Government icebreaker broke the ship out, but then became stuck herself. *Margaret Bowater* then broke her out, and led the little icebreaker into Corner Brook, much to the chagrin of the locals and the delight of the Bowater ship's crew.

Sadly, it was to be her turbines that led to *Margaret Bowater's* early demise, as although such machinery seemed never to wear out it proved very costly to run as fuel prices spiralled in the 1970s. Bowaters sold her in 1968, and a New York owner put her under the Liberian flag as *John W. Hill*. After becoming *Grand State* two years later, in June 1971 she arrived at Kaohsiung to be broken up at the ridiculously early age of 16.

Margaret Bowater running her trials

Completed in 1955 by William Denny and Brothers Ltd., Dumbarton.
6,481 gross tons, 419 feet overall.
Machinery: three Parsons geared turbines by William Denny and Brothers Ltd., Dumbarton reduction geared to a single shaft.

Margaret Bowater at Bowaters' Mill, Ellesmere Port is passed by the Shell tanker *Hadriana*

BRITISH HUSSAR

1962–1976

B.P. Tanker Co. Ltd., London

British Petroleum was appropriately named, as for much of its existence it was a nationalised body, and a very successful one. It was originally the Anglo-Persian Oil Co. Ltd. but was acquired by the British government in 1914 in order to assure fuel supplies for the Royal Navy's latest battleships, which were oil burning.

State ownership did not seem to fetter the company's ambition, and with the First World War over it laid plans to build the first oil refineries in the United kingdom at Swansea and Grangemouth, its oil previously having been processed at Abadan on the Persian Gulf. To feed these new refineries with crude, there began a massive expansion of its tanker fleet. The first British Hussar was one of 47 of the largest size of tanker built during the 1920s.

Until the late 1940s the largest vessel in the fleet was 12,250 tons deadweight, but thereafter an aggressive building programme led to ships of up to 35,000 tons entering the fleet. The second British Hussar, depicted here, and her sister British Cavalier were the last ships built for the company with accommodation amidships, as from 1965 to 1974 all-aft accommodation tankers of between 100,000 to 260,000 tons deadweight were constructed. David Kenwright considers the 1960s built tankers with mid-ships accommodation were perhaps the most aesthetically pleasing and best outfitted vessels ever built by the company.

David joined the company in 1965, its golden jubilee year, when the fleet totalled 97 vessels with a total deadweight of 2,650,572 tons. After three years at college, and six months working in heavy industry, he was more than ready to join his first ship. He signed on the British Hussar as an engineer cadet at the Finnart Oil Terminal in Loch Long in August 1969 sailing later that day for the Persian Gulf.

As the vessel steamed south, cargo tank cleaning was begun using mobile Butterworth machines, with scale and solids being removed by hand; and soon the ship's complement had settled into a steady routine for the month-long voyage.

The officers lived in some style and comfort, with silver service in the saloon: the six cadets all with large appetites often working through the menu without missing a course. In those days, alcohol was permitted aboard vessels, but cadets were officially allowed only two cans of beer a week each, although they were often given beer by the other officers, so did not fare too badly.

However, it was not always so pleasant, and David's first reality check came when there was a superheated steam leak in one of the boilers. The oil burners were withdrawn, and the air trunking and furnace access doors removed. Almost immediately, someone had to enter the furnace, head swathed in towels, and with a rag tied to a brush pole to locate the leaking tube, as superheated steam is invisible. That someone was David and, as he entered the furnace, he had grave doubts about surviving the ordeal.

The high point in the trip was to call at Cape Town for mail, fresh provisions and South African wine, which were brought out to the vessel in the bay. After a further uneventful couple of weeks British Hussar arrived at Abadan in the Persian Gulf, to load a cargo of crude oil. It was here they had their only run ashore, to the seaman's mission.

Electrician Murray Smith recalls some B.P. tankers having an Indian crew. The size of such a crew, twice that of a European one, meant the engineering officers had less to do. For instance, towards the end of each watch, the log had to be completed, which entailed checking every gauge and dipping each tank with a stick marked in feet and inches. With an Indian crew, the boilerman and oilman would do much of this work for the engineers, who only had to record the readings. Their precision at taking the readings was not matched by their precision with the English language, however. Murray remembers a man on his watch would call out 'number four tank, four feet, half past eleven!' when he meant four feet and eleven and a half inches.

British Hussar had a very short life, largely as a result of the changing pattern of the crude oil trade and the Suez Canal closure. She was demolished at Kaoshiung in January 1975, just before the fourteenth anniversary of her launch.

Completed in 1962 by John Brown and Co. Ltd., Clydebank.
32,341 gross tons, 760 feet.
Machinery: two steam turbines by John Brown and Co. Ltd., Clydebank, direct geared to a single shaft.

British Hussar. [J. & M. Clarkson]

British Hussar off Cape Town

WOODARRA

1957–1968

British India Steam Navigation Co. Ltd., London

British India had an extensive network of services round the Indian Ocean, and a share of the UK-Australia trade. In post-Second World War years, the latter business was important enough for the company to forsake the building of rather staid-looking split superstructure cargo liners for a modern, powerful and fast design. The turbine-driven and partly-refrigerated 'N' class appeared between 1954 and 1956, the four units achieving impressive speeds of over 18 knots on trial. But the company wanted to go farther, and developed the design into the *Woodarra* and her sister *Waroonga*. The 'N' class had been given place names from India, but the two 'W's took Australian names: Woodarra was a mine in Western Australia and Waroonga a small settlement in Queensland. They were a few feet longer and beamier than the 'Ns', but had one hatch fewer.

With no reefer space, and speeds of up to 21 knots, the ships were specifically intended for the annual 'wool derby', bringing the first of the season's wool clip to northern Europe. The ships' enlarged funnels, although they had no effect on performance, certainly suggested power, and this was available in abundance: turbines rated at 10,850 shaft horsepower were supplied with steam at 565 pounds per square inch and at 850° Fahrenheit. As the late Bill Laxon, historian of British India wrote, when pushed these ships could show a clean pair of heels to anything in the company's fleet.

Ian Stacey was a cadet on *Woodarra* during a voyage in 1958 and recalls her as an excellent ship on which to learn the ins and outs of how to become an officer. She was always meticulously maintained, any blemishes repaired at the earliest opportunity, and rotas laid down for every job. The crew were obviously very proud of her.

Woodarra was an exciting ship, too, and always the powerful forward surge of her engines could be felt. According to Ian she never seemed slowed by heavy seas, and in a long swell gave the impression of swimming like a dolphin. Cross seas, such as

encountered in the Bay of Biscay, could be uncomfortable, but even in such conditions she inspired confidence in the young and inexperienced seafarers who were her cadets. At sea *Woodarra* was rarely overtaken.

The cadets got the dirty jobs, as always, such as steam cleaning the Thermotank filters and, once cargo had been unloaded in Sydney, cleaning out the holds and bilges – an excellent way to learn how the ship was constructed, recalls Ian. And then there were the simply boring jobs: propeller watch as the turbines were kept turning gently during short stays in port; and searchlight duty in the heat of the Suez Canal.

In 1968 the prospect of the UK-Australia services becoming containerised meant that the *Woodarra* and *Waroonga* were transferred to the fleet of British India's parent, P&O. Because of closure of the Suez Canal, P&O's service between the UK and the Far East had been re-routed via the Panama Canal, and so the speed of the sisters was invaluable. *Woodarra* was given the unappealing name *Pando Gulf*, and ran for six years in this service before it too succumbed to the mighty box. With the introduction of the big 'Tokyo Bay' class containerships on Far East services, the British lines trading to the area agreed that all non-container cargo would be carried by Ben Line ships, and the

Woodarra as Pando Gulf, with P&O's black funnel. [J. & M. Clarkson]

former *Woodarra* was transferred in 1974 and renamed *Benalbanach*. With the end of even this residual trade, there was little work left for fast but expensive-to-run conventional cargo liners, and she went to breakers at Inchon, South Korea in May 1978.

The career of *Waroonga* ran almost in parallel with that of her sister. Transfer to P&O saw her become *Pando Point*, and in Ben colours she ran as *Benwyvis*. She was sold to breakers slightly earlier, however, arriving at Kaohsiung in January 1978.

Completed in 1957 by Barclay, Curle and Co. Ltd., Glasgow.
8,753 gross tons, 520 feet.
Machinery: Pametrada steam turbines by Barclay, Curle and Co. Ltd., Glasgow.

Woodarra at Adelaide

CHANTALA
1950–1971
British India Steam Navigation Co. Ltd., London

Just prior to of the Second World War, British India planned to build a new class of fast, diesel-driven cargo liners for their longer-distance routes, in particular those between the Persian Gulf and Australia. The outbreak of war delayed their building, and resulted in some modifications to the design, and the first to emerge was the twin-screw *Canara* in 1942. The 'C' group was eventually to comprise 13 British India ships, with two others going to other fleets within the P&O parent group. Later ships had modifications, including single screws, as it was felt wasteful in wartime to fit two valuable engines into one hull, as had been necessary with the early pair of twin-screw ships.

The most famous ships of this group were the *Chantala* and *Chindwara*, the culmination of British India's policy of having dedicated cadet ships. Each carried 38 cadets, originally in twin-berth and, for senior cadets, single-berth cabins which had originally been intended for seamen, whose work was to be done by the cadets. Initially, both ships usually ran to Australia and New Zealand from British ports on services operated by other P&O companies, including the New Zealand Shipping Co. Ltd.

As all new British India officers passed through *Chantala* or *Chindwara*, the ships became very well known, although the historians of the company note that 'it must be acknowledged that their popularity increased with distance from them'. In any case, their popularity nose-dived in 1959 when their capacity for cadets was increased to 52 through the addition of a 14-berth dormitory. At the same time a change was made from sailings to Australia to employment on routes to East and South Africa and India. The loss of the much-prized cabins dealt a severe blow to cadet morale, record the historians, and this does not seem to have improved in 1966 when the complement of cadets fell to just 16. This last alteration resulted from a change in policy which recognised that the company was turning out cadets who were competent ordinary seamen rather than having the technical and management skills required by officers. From 1966, cadets spent only part of

their training on a cadet ship, and the concept of such ships was abandoned in 1971.

One who obviously did like the ships was D.A.K. Nelson, an engineer who stood by another 'C' type, *Chandpara*, whilst she was building and remained with her, latterly as chief engineer, until he retired around 1970. In 1965 he was made commodore, a rank in the Merchant Navy usually given to the longest serving captain or chief engineer in a fleet, and meaning a modest increase in pay.

A small but significant addition to *Chantala's* decoration was a representation of British India's Britannia crest on her bow, the first time that one of their ships had carried it. In his after-dinner speech following the launch of *Chantala*, Barclay, Curle's chairman made a special mention of this feature, noting that it was completed entirely by the yard's own men. It is not known whether he was making a point about working practices, but he did indicate that those involved in the badge's design and fabrication included the drawing office, the loftsmen who made the moulds, the platers, the smith's finishers who burned and trimmed the plates to shape, the welders who put the whole lot together, and the painters. If that many trades were required to make a badge, how many did it take to build a whole ship?

Chantala and *Chindwara* had long and relatively uneventful careers with British India, the only major mishap affecting *Chantala* was when she was rammed by the collier *Hudson Deep* in the outer reaches of the Thames in March 1969.

Both the former British India cadet ships were sold to Singapore owners in April 1971, *Chantala* running as *Kota Sentosa* for just three years before being broken up at Tientsin. Sold in the same year, *Chindwara* became *Kota Aman*, and was demolished at Hong Kong in October 1974.

Chantala on the Thames. *[J. & M. Clarkson]*

Completed in 1959 by Barclay, Curle and Co. Ltd., Glasgow.
7,132 gross tons, 485 feet.
Machinery: Doxford-type six-cylinder oil engine by Barclay, Curle and Co. Ltd., Glasgow.

Chantala at Sydney

DWARKA
1946–1982
British India Steam Navigation Co. Ltd., London

The Indian Ocean was the centre of the activities of British India, and perhaps their most celebrated service was the Persian Gulf mail. It was to outlive almost all the company's other services.

Dwarka was one of four ships built for the mail service soon after the Second World War, replacements which were badly needed as the surviving ships had been built before the First World War. The lead yard was that of Barclay, Curle, who were British India's preferred builder, and had built 60 ships for them since 1905. *Dwarka* was the odd-man-out, being built on the Tyne, but achieved fame as being the last survivor.

Once the four ships – *Dumra, Dwarka, Dara* and *Daressa* – were all in service, a weekly sailing was provided from Bombay. Ports of call were Karachi, Gwadur or Pasni, Muscat, Bandar Abbas, Sharjah or Dubai, Bahrein, Mena al Ahmadi for bunkers, Kuwait, Bushire, Khorramshahr and finally Basra, where the ship remained for several days before returning via the same ports. A round voyage took about three weeks, and at the end of each the ship spent a week in Bombay. It sounds more like a bus route than a shipping line, but was a vital part of the local transport network, providing not just for cargo but also for the many people from the Indian subcontinent who sought work in the Arabian Gulf. As well as a modest number of first- and second-class cabins, the ships carried over 1,500 deck passengers – a complement which required the boats to be double-banked.

A feature of the service was that pilfering of the ship's fresh water was rife at almost all ports en route, despite the ships' enormous water capacity. This lead to a loss of weight which threatened stability problems during the final stages of the voyage, and necessitated the ships carrying permanent stone ballast.

There were inevitably minor incidents on such voyages, but what happened to the *Dara* was nothing short of tragedy. Following her arrival off Dubai on 7th April 1961, a storm suddenly arose whilst she was working cargo. A Panamanian-registered cargo ship, *Zeus*, dragged her anchor and was driven into *Dara's* bows. The British India ship's master decided to take her out into deep water, and was heading back for Dubai the next day when there was a violent explosion amidships followed by a raging fire. *Dara* had to be abandoned, but despite rescue work by the British *Empire Guillemot* the death toll was large: at least 212, with the actual figure being in doubt as the total onboard was not known with any certainty. The *Dara* capsized and sank in shallow water, and was refloated, only to sink again in deeper water whilst under tow. There are conflicting theories about the cause of the disaster, with a bomb being blamed for the explosion, but there is no forensic evidence for this, nor has any organisation claimed responsibility.

The three other members of the 'D' class had more peaceful ends. The last built, *Daressa*, was the first to go, sold in 1964 to the Chandris organisation who intended converting her for cruising, but then sold her to Singapore owners, and she worked in south east Asia until 1974. *Dumra*, the first built, was chartered in 1972 to an Indian shipping company, as nationalism made it politically expedient to have a ship under a local flag. She was later sold to this company, and broken up in 1979.

Dwarka. [J. & M. Clarkson collection]

Dwarka, subject of the painting, was the longest to serve in British India ownership and indeed the longest lived of the quartet, surviving until 1982. She became something of a celebrity, attracting enthusiasts from the UK to make the voyage in one of her first or second class cabins, and even featuring in a television documentary. As the last ship in British India colours in the Indian Ocean, she was a a poignant reminder of the British raj.

Completed in 1947 by Swan, Hunter and Wigham Richardson Ltd., Wallsend-on-Tyne.
4,851 gross tons, 399 feet.
Machinery: Doxford-type five-cylinder oil engine by Swan, Hunter and Wigham Richardson Ltd., Wallsend-on-Tyne.

Dwarka in the Shatt-al-Arab waterway

EMPRESS OF SCOTLAND
1930–1958

Canadian Pacific Railway Company (Canadian Pacific Steamships Ltd., managers), Liverpool

During the course of a long and distinguished career, *Empress of Scotland*, as she became, sailed on Canadian Pacific's two major routes, across the Pacific and across the Atlantic.

Services across the Pacific were begun by the Canadian Pacific Railway almost as soon as its transcontinental railroad was completed between Montreal and Vancouver in the late 1880s. One of the incentives was to generate eastbound traffic on the railway, it being pointed out that goods from the Far East could reach the UK quicker via Canada than on P&O's sailings via the Suez Canal. However, a subsidy from the Canadian government was necessary before the company's first steamships, the Empresses, were introduced to the Pacific route in 1890.

On her completion in 1930, *Empress of Japan* was the finest and fastest vessel sailing out of Vancouver to the Far East, where she called at Yokohama and Hong Kong. Following the outbreak of war in 1939 she was quickly requisitioned as a troopship, a service on which she was to be engaged for nine years, and involved her steaming 600,000 miles. Only one untoward incident is recorded: in November 1940 she was attacked by aircraft off the coast of Ireland but managed to avoid damage. However, her name did not survive. Following the Japanese attack on Pearl Harbour and aggression in the Far East, there were complaints about her carrying the name *Empress of Japan*. Some minor bureaucratic difficulties had to be overcome, as there was a general prohibition on name changes during the war, but in October 1942 she became *Empress of Scotland*, the second of the name.

Such was the pressure on shipyards after the Second World War that it was not until May 1950 that *Empress of Scotland* completed her conversion for peacetime employment. Circumstances in the Far East precluded her resuming her former service, and instead she joined the company's North Atlantic services, running from Liverpool via Greenock to Quebec. For this, her previously open promenade deck was glassed in. Shortening of her masts in 1952 had a deleterious effect on her appearance, but allowed her to use Montreal as a terminal port. In winter when weather made crossing the Atlantic less popular, *Empress of Scotland* cruised from New York to the West Indies. The painting depicts her after her masts had been shortened.

Service on Canadian Pacific's North Atlantic ships was popular with seafarers, despite the rigours of the weather in winter. The voyages were relatively short, and Bill Cunningham recalls that, once he had accumulated four weeks' leave, he could take a voyage off. Another attraction was that Canadian Pacific had the reputation of being the highest paying British shipping company. Despite their being a Canadian company, their deep-sea ships were registered in, and crewed and run from, the United Kingdom.

With the new *Empress of Britain* and *Empress of England* coming into service in 1956 and 1957, *Empress of Scotland* was retired from Canadian Pacific service, but had much life left in her. Following work at Belfast and Hamburg which reduced her three funnels to two, she returned to the Atlantic as the German *Hanseatic*, in the ownership of the Hamburg Atlantic Line. Her route was now from Cuxhaven to New York, calling at Le Havre, Southampton and Cobh, carrying mainly tourist-class passengers. Sadly, her career was terminated in September 1966 by a fire at New York, which made repair of the 36-year old ship uneconomic, and she was towed across the Atlantic for demolition in Hamburg.

The small painting on this page depicts a one-time running mate, *Duchess of Richmond*, completed on the Clyde in 1929 for North Atlantic services. Following war service as a trooper, in 1947 this Duchess moved up the social hierarchy to become an Empress, complete with white hull, the *Empress of Canada*. In an odd parallel with what was to happen to *Empress of Scotland* many years later, the *Empress of Canada* caught fire on her berth in Liverpool's Gladstone Dock in January 1953. During fire fighting operations she capsized, giving a major problem to the port authorities. Eventually, after almost 18 months of endeavour, she was righted and removed from the dock and made sufficiently seaworthy for a last voyage to an Italian scrapyard.

Duchess of Richmond

Empress of Scotland
Completed in 1930 by the Fairfield Shipbuilding and Engineering Co. Ltd., Govan.
26,032 gross tons, 644 feet.
Machinery: six steam turbines by the Fairfield Shipbuilding and Engineering Co. Ltd., Govan, geared to two shafts.

Empress of Scotland westbound across the North Atlantic

SOOCHOW

1947–1967

China Navigation Co. Ltd. (John Swire and Sons Ltd.), London

John Swire was one of the greatest of Britain's merchant-shipowners. From his base in Liverpool he became convinced of the potential for trade with China, which was being opened up by various treaties forced on the country by the western powers. Crucially, Swire was an early investor in Alfred Holt's ships, and it was on one of these that Swire travelled to Shanghai in 1866, and realised that this city at the mouth of the Yangtse River was the key to immense trading possibilities. Swire established an office on the Shanghai Bund, initially to handle cotton consigned to Lancashire mills, but quickly became the agent for Holt's Blue Funnel Line. Swire was an important influence on Holt, persuading him to build faster ships and to inaugurate the Far East Freight Conference. However, when Holts refused to take an interest in trade up the Yangtse, Swire floated the China Navigation Co. Ltd. Not surprisingly with such an entrepreneur at its head, this company expanded far beyond its original ambitions, operating on routes along the China coast, with a network of services to Australia, the Philippines, and the islands of Indonesia. There were, however, enormous difficulties: at times China descended into civil war, and banditry and especially piracy affected the China Navigation ships. The weakness of government in this enormous country was exploited both by the Japanese, who invaded China in 1937, and by Mao Tse Tung's communists who, aided by Japan's defeat in 1945, completed their conquest of Mainland China in 1949.

Ten years of war had seriously reduced the fleet of China Navigation, and *Soochow* was the last of four ships ordered to replace the company's losses, and almost the last China coaster. A major advance in these ships was the installation of air conditioning, the outward signs of which were the lack of ventilators. The four ships were placed on a service from Shanghai to Hong Kong, calling at Tsingtao, Amoy and Swatow. However, with the Communist capture of Shanghai in 1949 and its subsequent blockade by opposing Nationalist forces based in Taiwan, this service became untenable.

In July 1953 *Soochow* joined the New Guinea Australia Line (NGAL). She was employed on six-to-seven-week round voyages from Sydney to Brisbane, Port Moresby, Samarai, Lae, Kavieng and Rabaul. The first ship in the area to be fitted with radar, *Soochow* was able to make night passages through island groups rather than round them, a practice that saved a lot of time. The competing line, Burns Philp, made no night sailings as a matter of practice. Charts of the area were inaccurate and many showed corrections made by the officers, which were then sent on to the British Admiralty. Names of China Navigation's ships often appeared amongst the weekly Notices to Mariners. Along the coast from Madang to Lae there was no overlap by British Admiralty charts and the gap was covered by an Australian chart issued in 1945 on which was a note that the marine survey was carried out by the US Navy and the land survey by the Australian Army. As a result of the different surveys the coastline appeared stretched and the *Soochow* always increased speed on this chart to fourteen knots! On one Admiralty chart was the legend 'Reefs seen by D'Entrecasteaux 1792'.

Terry Connell joined *Soochow* as Second Mate in December 1957. During his first six months she usually carried almost a full cargo to Port Moresby, consisting of stores and equipment for an oil exploration company, plus some 300 tons to Samarai. It was a delightful period for the ship's officers, consisting of five days minimum turn-round in Sydney, two days in Brisbane and four in Port Moresby, but it came to an end when the explorers moved on having failed to find commercial quantities of oil. The full voyage schedule was then resumed, the turn-round port now being Melbourne. During 1960 a call was made to Honiara, Solomon Islands, with general cargo and to load logs floated out from the coast just east of the port. The approach to the anchorage was along a line of soundings obtained by the agent in Rabaul from a Burns Philp ship. Industrial espionage was at work there!

Loading was an interesting challenge to the chief officer as the break-bulk cargo was loaded in three ports and was discharged in five or six. He also had to make sure that vehicles for each port were on top of cargo for the same port of discharge and create space for the occasional southbound load of logs and or rubber. The principal export from the islands, copra, was a monopoly of Burns Philp, hence voyages southbound were light ship and sometimes against head winds, at slow speeds to reduce pounding, especially through Bass Strait to Melbourne.

Until the introduction of pressurized aircraft on services between Australia and the islands, the ships' passenger accommodation was frequently full but latterly not, though some people did the round voyage as a cruise. When there were more than 12 a delightful retired Australian doctor in his eighties was signed on. He could hardly say that his duty was arduous as healthiness was a requirement for life in Papua New Guinea. Hangovers and seasickness were the only familiar ailments.

The heavy-lift derrick was in occasional use as it had the greatest lift capability of all the ships in the area at that time. After *Soochow*'s eight-year survey it was down-graded from 25 to 20 tons but was still of great practical use for such things as a Caterpillar bulldozer for Lae, a road-building scraper and bulldozer for Madang and a boxed helicopter for Port Moresby.

By 1964 ships like *Soochow* were not covering their costs and drastic changes were made to routes. By 1967 new cargo handling methods were introduced and the ship was sold in July to Pacific International Lines who renamed her *Kota Ratu*. She had one more, rather unexpected, career change when sold to Malaysia in 1975. As *Sang Fajar* she was apparently civilian owned, but used as a troop ship. This prolonged her life well beyond that of her sisters, and she was not broken up until June 1984.

China Navigation remains an important shipping concern, but it is only one of the Swire Group's massively diversified interests in industry, property and transportation. Perhaps one of its biggest successes is Cathay Pacific, one of the world's most profitable airlines, an enterprise of which John Swire would undoubtedly have approved.

Completed in 1947 by A. and J. Inglis Ltd., Glasgow.
3,152 gross tons, 321 feet.
Machinery: three-cylinder oil engine by William Doxford and Sons Ltd., Sunderland.

Soochow at Port Moresby

CLAN MENZIES

1958–1979

China Navigation Co. Ltd. (John Swire and Sons Ltd.), London

The *Clan Menzies* was the last conventional cargo liner built for Clan Line with accommodation squarely amidships. In subsequent designs, the superstructure moved to the three-quarters aft position, losing some of the classic elegance of the earlier design. The design of the *Clan Menzies* and her sisters *Clan Malcolm* and *Clan Matheson* was clearly based on the turbine steamers *Clan Robertson* of 1954 and *Clan Ross* of 1956 with the addition of a pair of kingposts on the poop. As in the steamers, accommodation was trunked around the number four hold. This may not have been popular with the crew allocated such cabins, as sleep must have been disturbed whilst cargo was being worked at this hold. Being motor ships, *Clan Menzies* and her sisters did not require the cowl-topped funnel which was such a very distinctive feature of their steamer predecessors. Nevertheless, they were handsome ships, with a particularly elegant rounded stern.

Clan Menzies was the 22nd new ship delivered to Clan Line since the Second World War, and joined a fleet which still included wartime standard ships. Together, they maintained sailings principally from Vittoria Dock, Birkenhead and King George V Dock, Glasgow to South and East Africa, India, Pakistan, Ceylon and Australia. Outward they carried manufactured goods and sometimes bulk cargoes such as china clay from Fowey, and almost always cargo included consignments of Scotch whisky. Clan Line also specialised in heavy loads such as railway rolling stock and locomotives, buses and heavy machinery, and had one of its ships, *Clan Sutherland*, specially equipped with a 165-ton derrick. Homeward cargoes typically comprised copper and tobacco from Africa; from India and Pakistan tea, oilcake, manganese ore, cotton and other fibres, and cashew nuts; and from Australia wool and meat in the refrigerated vessels. Discharge was usually at Tilbury, Avonmouth, Liverpool and Manchester, usually finishing in Glasgow, often for a spell in dry dock. To reach Manchester the topmasts, and sometimes the funnel top would have to be removed to allow passage beneath the bridges on the Manchester Ship Canal.

John Howell spent 15 years as an engineer with the company, and recalls that the deck,

Clan Menzies running trials on the Clyde

engine room and catering ratings on Clan Line ships were often recruited either in Calcutta or in Chittagong, which is now in Bangladesh but was then part of East Pakistan. Those from Calcutta usually spoke good English, but not those from Chittagong, and use had to be made of a sort of *lingua franca* called Lascari bat. Catering staff from the Indian sub-continent always prepared a very authentic curry for the main meal each day, something which was much sought after by visitors to the ship.

Despite Clan Line's strong Clydeside connections, deck and engineering officers came not just from Scotland but from all over of the UK. However, when in Glasgow the locals did enjoy a perk. In all other UK ports, the crew were expected to turn to and begin work at 7.00 am, stopping for breakfast at 8.30 am. However, when working cargo in Glasgow 'turn to' time was not until breakfast was over at 9.30 am, to allow those living locally to get back from a night at home. John recalls that some superintendents could be very particular in observing the 7.00 am turn to. Returning to one ship after his leave he found that his relief had been sacked, having been found in his bed after 7.00 am!

Clan Menzies and her sisters each gave Clan Line 21 years' service, but only *Clan Menzies* had anything of a subsequent career. In 1979 she was sold and renamed *Trinity Splendour*. *Clan Malcolm* went to the same Hong Kong-based owners as *Trinity Fair* but she made only one voyage out to the Far East where she was broken up. In contrast, the former *Clan Menzies*, although due to be broken up, was sold to China Ocean Shipping Company and traded as *Xing Long*. Where she was eventually broken up is not known, as China has remained an area where a ship can be demolished with no one from the west aware of it, and *Lloyd's Register* deleted her for lack of up-to-date information in October 1992.

Completed in 1958 by Greenock Dockyard Co. Ltd., Greenock.
7,315g, gross tons, 503 feet.
Machinery: Doxford-type six-cylinder oil engine by Wallsend Slipway and Engineering Co. Ltd., Wallsend-on-Tyne.

Clan Menzies at Zanzibar

MAURETANIA
1906–1935
Cunard Steamship Co. Ltd., Liverpool

Mauretania and her ill-fated sister *Lusitania* are two of the most celebrated North Atlantic liners, their careers encompassing both triumph and tragedy. They were triumphs of naval architecture and engineering, their machinery being 75% more powerful than anything built previously. They were also the first ships to exceed 30,000 tons, and the first with quadruple screws. Their building was in response to the challenges posed by Norddeutscher Lloyd's blue-ribband winning *Kronprinz Wilhelm* and *Kaiser Wilhelm II*, and by the US-based International Mercantile Marine, which was bent on dominating transatlantic shipping and had recently acquired control of Cunard's arch-rival, the White Star Line.

The *Mauretania* was also responsible for the formation of one of the giants of British shipbuilding. Being able to bid for this large and highly prestigious contract was a decisive factor in the merger of C.S. Swan and Hunter and J. Wigham Richardson. There were great technical obstacles to be overcome, and human ones too: Charles Parsons had to convince the Cunard board that his turbines would give the ships the performance required, rather than quadruple-expansion steam reciprocating engines the board favoured. Perhaps not surprisingly with such a leap forward, both hull and machinery cost much more than estimated.

The performance of the ships was also a triumph. *Mauretania* was the faster of the two, probably thanks to improvements made in the light of experience with her sister. In 1909, after three years in service, she crossed the Atlantic at an average speed of just over 26 knots, and remained the fastest ship on this ocean until 1929.

The building of the two ships had been subsidised by the British government, the reason given being that the Royal Navy would use them as auxiliary cruisers in time of war. When the war did break out in 1914, however, they were rejected for this role as being too large and fuel-hungry, so either the Admiralty were unusually stupid, or the government dishonest. *Mauretania*'s war service was arduous, but completed in safety, despite involving three voyages to Gallipoli as a troopship, service as a hospital ship, and finally carrying troops across the Atlantic. Not so her sister ship, of course, which was torpedoed by the German submarine *U 20* on 7th May 1915 whilst in the Irish Sea. This was something of an own goal for

Germany, if such a sporting simile can be applied to tragic loss of almost 1,200 passengers and crew on the *Lusitania*, as it helped sway public opinion in neutral countries towards the Allied cause and helped gain the decisive involvement of the United States on the Allied side. The Germans badly mishandled the propaganda surrounding this sinking, and the medal they struck to commemorate it was copied and widely distributed by the British to demonstrate the supposed callousness of their enemy.

Mauretania's performances improved with age, and a refit in 1921 which saw her converted from coal to oil firing increased her speed. In August 1929, when her 1909 record had just been beaten by the *Bremen*, the 22-year-old ship gamely attempted to regain the blue ribband, and achieved a personal best of 26.9 knots westbound and 27.2 eastbound. Given such a performance, it is sad that from 1930 the state of the North Atlantic passenger trade meant that *Mauretania* was mainly employed cruising, her hull later being painted white for this role. She was sold to breakers in 1935 and, in July made her way to Rosyth under her own steam, pausing briefly off the river of her birth. The Geordies had an enormous pride in this superb example of Tyneside shipbuilding, and Hylton Charlton recalls being taken to see her as an eight-year old child: 'As *Mauretania* passed the mouth of the Tyne, they brought her in as close as they could to the shore in order that she and the people who built her might pay their last respects, one to the other.' As she moved slowly north passed St. Mary's Island '...my father and dozens of other fully grown men around me wept openly... I had never seen a grown-up man cry before, and I cannot remember ever seeing my father cry again ... that day, he was surrounded by dozens of men whose faces were as wet with tears as his'.

Before *Mauretania* left Southampton on her final voyage, the shipbreakers arranged an auction of her fittings which yielded almost £15,000. Brass letters from the name on her port bow fetched £15 each, and there were even takers for coat hangers carrying her name. Somewhere, large and small pieces of one of the most famous and successful express liners must still survive.

Mauretania. [B. & A. Fielden]

Completed in 1906 by Swan, Hunter and Wigham Richardson Ltd., Newcastle-upon-Tyne. 31,938 gross tons, 762 feet.
Machinery: four Parsons steam turbines by the Wallsend Slipway Co. Ltd., Wallsend-on-Tyne.

Mauretania at Southampton

BERENGARIA

1922–1938

Cunard Steamship Co. Ltd., Liverpool

This ship was built to re-establish the status of a German line, but ended up enhancing the standing of one of its greatest rivals, such were the fortunes of war.

As *Imperator* she was the first of three ships planned by Albert Ballinn, the inspired head of Hamburg-Amerika Line, which in size and luxury would eclipse those of White Star, Cunard and German rivals Norddeutscher Lloyd. As the competitors included the *Olympic* and *Aquitania*, the German ships had to be something special. To ensure their profitable operation, Ballinn needed a mail contract from the German government, but he had taken the precaution of involving the Kaiser in the planning, and the ruler's enthusiasm for this prestigious project helped sway the government over the mail contract. It also affected the naming, and instead of the intended title *Europa*, she became *Imperator*. Ballinn's architects and designers modelled the *Imperator*'s internal fittings on those of French eighteenth-century chateaux, a neglect of German style which had its critics. As well as her sheer size, she had one of the most monstrous figureheads ever carried. This depicted a giant eagle wearing an imperial crown, perched on, or perhaps clutching, a large globe with the legend 'Mein Feld ist Die Weld', literally 'my field is the world.' Although appropriate for a large liner about to set out to conquer the world, given the imperial rivalries which were shortly to erupt into the First World War, it could be interpreted as an expression of the German nation's ambition. Most of the figurehead was removed by an Atlantic storm in 1914.

At the time of her entry into service in June 1913, *Imperator* was by a small margin the largest ship in the world. However, her debut was not auspicious, as on her maiden voyage it became apparent that she was top heavy and lacking stability, and she had a distressing tendency to catch fire, which bedevilled her throughout her career. Ballinn described her as 'a first class hotel but a third class ship'. She was sent back to her builders for remedial work in November 1913, and was out of operation until March 1914, emerging with 2,000 tons of cement in her double bottom.

The armistice in 1918 saw all German ships over 1,800 tons surrendered to the Allies. *Imperator* went initially to the USA as a naval transport, but eventually was ceded to Britain. Cunard and rivals White Star jointly bought *Imperator* and the *Bismarck*. *Imperator* was refitted on the Tyne, converted to oil burning and in February 1921 was renamed *Berengaria*.

Berengaria joined *Aquitania* and *Mauretania* on Cunard's express service, and initially did well, not

least because the war had temporarily removed German competition from the North Atlantic. However, it was not to last.

Amongst the facilities on *Berengaria* was a brokerage room, where shares could be bought and sold by radio telegraph. During 1929 the ship's daily news-sheet warned of selling pressures on the New York Stock Exchange. Alerted by that night's news-sheet, most of the first class passengers rushed to the brokerage and began selling shares. However, second class passengers, who included many with shares, were initially not allowed access to the brokerage which was in the first class area, the master Captain Rostron not permitting company rules to be broken in this way. Such was the panic, however, that a few second-class passengers were allowed through, passed back details of prices for others, and relayed selling instructions.

The stock exchange crash meant that things were never the same again on *Berengaria*. Her Atlantic crossings slumped to 12 in 1930, and just 10 in 1931. However, she did some cruising from New York, with the attraction that being a British ship, prohibition did not prevail on board. The low point came in September 1932 when one eastbound crossing had only 134 passengers. After that, helped by fare reductions and cuts in crew wages, things improved slowly, although the ship continued to lose money. She also lost her place as Cunard's flagship, as following the merger with White Star which was part of the price of a government loan to complete the *Queen Mary*, the newer and slightly bigger *Majestic* took that honour.

With *Queen Mary* in service and *Queen Elizabeth* on order, time was running out for *Berengaria* in the late 1930s. She might have survived longer but for a prolonged series of electrical fires caused by her aged wiring. These became so frequent that the United States Steamboat Inspection Service withdrew her passenger certificate in 1938. *Berengaria* was sent to Jarrow for demolition and by September 1939 her hull had been cut down to waterline. However, with more urgent work, demolition was not completed until she was towed to Rosyth in 1946.

She had promised great things, but historical circumstances, abetted by some constructional weaknesses, meant *Imperator/Berengaria* was never to achieve the success her designers intended.

Berengaria laid up at Southampton. [J. & M. Clarkson collection]

Completed in 1913 by Vulkan Werke, Hamburg. 52,226 gross tons, 884 feet.
Machinery: four steam turbines by Vulkan Werke, Hamburg.

Berengaria at New York

SCYTHIA

1920–1958

Cunard Steamship Co. Ltd., Liverpool

The Cunard fleet was much depleted during the First World War, and an ambitious rebuilding programme was necessary if the line was to re-establish its position. Although it had lost the *Lusitania* during the war, Cunard gained another express liner in the shape of the German-built *Berengaria*, and so with the *Mauretania* and *Aquitania* surviving there was no need for another big ship. Reconstruction therefore concentrated on the intermediate ships, of which no fewer than 13 were built to three different sizes between 1920 and 1925.

First of the new programme was *Scythia*, one of an eventual total of five 20,000 tonners, and intended for services to New York and Boston. Her delivery was not without difficulties, however, as a strike of joiners at Barrow threatened to seriously delay her fitting out, so she was sent to Lorient in France to be completed. She was followed to two sisters, *Samaria* and *Laconia*. The three could be distinguished from two later ships of the same size, *Franconia* and *Carinthia*, by the break in the two uppermost decks abaft the bridge, a feature which gave these ships a somewhat anachronistic appearance.

Scythia was requisitioned as a troop transport almost immediately on the outbreak of war in August 1939. She had a narrow escape at Algiers after the Operation Torch landings in November 1942 when hit by a aerial torpedo, but was repaired and returned to trooping. Her sister *Samaria* also came through the war, but not the *Laconia*, which became one of the most tragic losses on the Allied side during the Second World War.

By September 1942 *Laconia* was a troop transport following a spell as an armed merchant cruiser, and was off Freetown, Sierra Leone with a complement of some 2,500, including 1,800 Italian prisoners-of-war, when torpedoed by the German submarine *U 156*. Although there were sufficient boats and life rafts to accommodate all 2,500, many could not be launched because of *Laconia's* list and, to add to their suffering, survivors in the water were attacked by sharks. Realising what a tragedy he had unleashed the submarine commander, Kapitan-Leutnant Hartenstein, began rescue work and radioed a request to other U-boats to come to the scene. Although he broadcast a message in English suggesting a cease-fire whilst rescue operations were underway, Hartenstein's boat was attacked by a US Liberator aircraft, despite the submarine displaying a red cross flag. Further air attacks on rescue craft followed. In response, a disgusted Admiral Doenitz, head of U-boat operations, issued the 'Laconia Order' which reinforced previous instructions that submarine commanders were not to risk their boats and operations by rescuing survivors. After the war, the order was produced in evidence during Doenitz' trial for war crimes at Nuremburg, but this had little effect. Given the situation surrounding the sinking of *Laconia*, it is perhaps remarkable that at least one thousand people were rescued.

After the war the two survivors of the class, *Scythia* and *Samaria*, were returned to service, the former being given a lengthy refit in 1949-1950 at Clydebank. She then sailed out of Southampton, mainly to Quebec, but occasionally ran to New York when deputising for one of the Queens during their annual overhauls. *Scythia* was withdrawn following the arrival of new ships, and broken up on the Forth during 1958. She had completed 38 years of strenuous service.

Scythia sails from Malta during a post-war trooping voyage. *[Ships in Focus]*

Completed in 1920 by Vickers Ltd., Barrow-in-Furness.
19,730 gross tons, 624 feet.
Machinery: six steam turbines by Vickers Ltd., Barrow-in-Furness, double-reduction geared to twin shafts.

Scythia at Liverpool

QUEEN MARY

1936–1967

Cunard White Star Ltd., Liverpool

The ship which came to represent British shipping at its zenith was the result of woeful circumstances. In the late 1920s, Cunard had three fine but elderly liners on its North Atlantic express service out of Southampton, *Aquitania*, *Mauretania* and *Berengaria*, and was feeling the results of competition from newer ships. But at the depth of the economic depression, Cunard did not have the resources to replace them. White Star, Britain's other major line on the North Atlantic, was in a similar position with old ships and even more penurious circumstances with its membership of Kylsant's collapsed Royal Mail Group.

In 1930 Cunard went ahead and placed an order at Clydebank for the first of what it hoped would be two 80,000-ton ships. In public, the company expressed disdain for the blue ribband, but the new ship, known simply by its yard number 834, was clearly intended to take the record from its current holder, the German *Bremen*. However, with economic conditions worsening, Cunard ordered work to stop on 834 at the end of 1931, and her rusting hull became the symbol of failed economic policies and unemployment that characterised much of the interwar years. The French, building the rival *Normandie* at the same time, had the sense to continue with their work.

In 1934 the British government acted and advanced Cunard a loan of £3,000,000 to complete 834, foreseeing that even more would be needed if a sister was ever to be built. A condition of the loan was that Cunard and White Star would merge, Cunard being seen as the company that could best help the government unscramble the mess in which White Star had been left. The restart of work on 834 was symbolic of a determination, at last, to aid economic recovery.

As *Queen Mary*, yard number 834 was launched by H.M. Queen Mary in September 1934. A story is told that Cunard wished to continue with their traditional naming scheme and call her *Victoria*, and hence asked King George V if the ship could be named after 'the greatest British queen'. 'Of course', the king is reputed to have said, 'my wife would be delighted to have a ship named after her.' Cunard historians deny this, and claim that her three predecessors were referred to in contemporary publicity material as 'the Queens of the North Atlantic' and the name for the new ship reflected this. Whatever the truth, her name became a byword for stateliness and size,

and many things large and grand, including humble buses and lorries, have been dubbed 'Queen Mary'.

The delay in completion allowed the *Normandie* to take the lead, and on her maiden voyage in May 1935 she set a new Atlantic record. Although the speeds achieved on her trials indicated that *Queen Mary* could outrun the French ship, Cunard were initially cautious. Following her maiden voyage in May 1936 she was allowed to settle down for a few voyages before taking the record in August. *Normandie* then regained it, but *Queen Mary* recaptured the blue riband in 1938 with record crossings both east and west bound.

The war service of *Queen Mary* and her slightly larger consort *Queen Elizabeth* is well known, when their speed and capacity to carry troops made them immensely useful and, history suggests, almost invulnerable to U-boat attack. However, in October 1942 the *Queen Mary* contributed to a tragedy when she cut in two the escorting cruiser *HMS Curacoa* which sank almost instantly.

The post-war years were dog days for the two Queens, and in truth there was nothing to challenge them on the North Atlantic until the *United States* made her dramatic debut in 1952. Even then, the Queens with their scheduled weekly sailings continued to attract much business. It was not until the late 1960s that airline competition virtually killed the market for Atlantic passenger ships. There was almost as much angst around Cunard's deliberations about replacing the two Queens as had surrounded the original decision to build them, and a third large queen was seriously proposed (dubbed 'Q3' by contemporary journalists). But sense prevailed, and the result was the scaled down *Queen Elizabeth 2* ('Q4' for a time, before becoming 'QE2'), a ship better suited to cruising with occasional line voyages.

In 1967 *Queen Mary* was sold to the city of Long Beach, California. She remains there today, having spent more years as a maritime museum than she did on the North Atlantic.

Completed in 1936 by John Brown and Co. Ltd., Clydebank.
81,235 gross tons, 975 feet.
Machinery: sixteen steam turbines by John Brown and Co. Ltd., Clydebank, single reduction geared to four shafts.

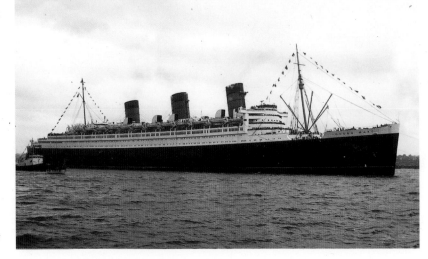

Queen Mary at Southampton. [Roy Fenton collection]

Queen Mary at sea

BRITANNIC

1930–1957

Oceanic Steam Navigation Co. Ltd. (White Star Line) Liverpool
Cunard White Star Ltd., Liverpool

The motor liners *Britannic* and her later and less fortunate sister *Georgic* were the somewhat muted swan song of one of the great North Atlantic companies, White Star Line.

White Star's troubles had begun in April 1912 when its newest ship had been so badly navigated that it came off worse in an encounter with several million tons of ice. Disaster was turned into tragedy because the owners had, unaccountably, forgotten to buy enough life-saving equipment for all classes of passenger. It is often forgotten that White Star was US-owned at this period, being controlled since 1902 by the financier J. Pierpoint Morgan as part of his International Mercantile Marine Company. Morgan's grandiose plans of domination of the North Atlantic trade were never achieved, and after the First World War he lost interest and decided to sell his ships, but was prevented by political interference. Much of White Star's one time prestige had been lost in the *Titanic* disaster, and it operated a somewhat motley fleet in post war years. But not until 1927, when North Atlantic services had been hit by depression and restrictions on US emigration, was White Star sold, becoming part of Kylsant's Royal Mail Group. Celebrations of its return to British control were short-lived, as Royal Mail was itself a basket case, victim of the recession and Kylsant's creative accountancy practices. Unscrambling the omelette that Kylsant had created took the government some time, and its quandary over what to do with White Star was solved with a forcible merger with rival Cunard, who were persuaded to agree by being given a generous subsidy to enable them to complete the *Queen Mary*.

One positive result of Royal Mail ownership of White Star was the ordering of *Britannic* and *Georgic*. The Royal Mail group had rightly favoured motor ships, which offered major economies over steamships. The completion of these two motor liners marked a definite break with White Star traditions, which their very squat funnels seemed to emphasis. The pair were, in fact, less modest than they appeared. Although no first class passengers were carried, their accommodation for 480 cabin class passengers was of a very high standard. They

were the first diesel-driven passenger ships on the North Atlantic and, but for a solitary Italian vessel, the biggest motor ships yet built. After 1935, when the pair were used on a service from London via Southampton and Le Havre to New York, the *Georgic* became the largest ship to regularly use the Thames. And with a 1933 Atlantic crossing at an average of 19½ knots, *Britannic* was no slouch. It is reported that her engine room was so cool that radiators had to be fitted.

Both ships were requisitioned as troop carriers during the Second World War. *Britannic* seems to have had no untoward experiences in this role, but *Georgic* was almost destroyed. In July 1941 she was bombed and set on fire whilst at anchor at Port Tewfik, Egypt, and was beached, burnt out and half submerged. It was decided to salvage and repair her, but this was a very protracted operation, involving towing the hulk to Bombay in order to make it sufficiently seaworthy to return to the UK for reconditioning, which was completed only in December 1944. Owners were now the British government, and she was used initially as a troopship, although in 1948 her accommodation was refitted to make it slightly more comfortable for emigrants when she was not troop carrying. Now looking decidedly cut down, with just one funnel and one mast, *Georgic* went unmourned to the breakers in 1956.

Britannic, however, was refitted as a passenger ship in 1948 and was placed on Cunard's Liverpool to New York service, being sufficiently smart to offer cruises from New York to the Caribbean in the winter. The writer of these captions can offer a personal recollection of her: as a teenager in December 1960 he visited the Mersey to see what was then the last ship wearing White Star colours conclude her final voyage. It was the end of a long and eventful chapter in the history of British shipping.

Georgic in the Mersey

Completed in 1930 by Harland and Wolff Ltd., Belfast. 26,943 gross tons, 217 feet.
Machinery: two Burmeister & Wain-type ten-cylinder oil engines by Harland and Wolff Ltd., Belfast, driving twin shafts.

Britannic at Liverpool

ALSATIA

1951 – 1963

Cunard Steamship Co. Ltd., Liverpool

Although best known for their passenger ships, Cunard also operated a number of cargo ships on both its North Atlantic and Mediterranean services. The years after the Second World War saw its cargo fleet at its largest and most interesting, with a varied collection of new and second-hand ships. The latter included two impressive, twin-funnelled, turbine steamers. They had been ordered by S.J. Thompson and Company, whose family also owned the Sunderland yard in which they were built, as part of ambitious plans to expand their Silver Line fleet. As *Silverplane* and *Silverbriar* they were intended for a round-the-world service, for which their three turbines drove them at a creditable 16 knots. But the service did not prosper and the pair was acquired by Cunard in 1951. *Silverplane* became *Alsatia* and operated largely on the London, Le Havre and New York service. The two-funnel profile was unique for pure cargo ships in post-war years, and gave them a distinction amongst the shipping fraternity.

Placed right forward on the bridge, the forward funnel could not have served the boilers of these turbine-driven ships, and was in fact a dummy accommodating the radar equipment, the monkey island, chart room, radio room, wheel house and quarters for both the master and a pilot. The large superstructure had excellent accommodation for officers, but Alan Phipps recalls that the seamen and engine room crew were still accommodated in the poop. However, these grades regarded Cunard as a good company, giving it the ultimate accolade 'a good feeder'.

Not being built for a heavy weather route, when used on the North Atlantic the ships needed some reinforcement. The most visible of these were six-foot plates welded at the forward corners of the superstructure which joined the bulwarks to the deck. Almost useless, these developed such substantial cracks that in bad weather it was said 'they're cracking walnuts in those split plates.'

Adverse weather could drive the ships well to the south of their normal route, and Alan recalls being nearer to Madeira than to Merseyside when, on taking over the wheel, he was amazed to see the propeller wash appearing ahead of the bow, so strong were the head seas. He also had the helm once during an unaccustomed transit of the narrow Chesapeake Canal, when the master enquired of him whether he had ever been there before. Despite a negative response, Alan was left to it, his reward for not demolishing bridges, jetties or other craft being a tot of the captain's whisky.

Cargoes westbound included manufactured goods, cars, chemicals and Scotch whisky. Eastbound they were timber products, paper, asbestos and maize, the last-named in deep tanks originally intended for liquid cargoes. Westbound these tanks were sealed after being filled with London dock water as ballast, and this left its distinctive aroma, as did any residual rotting grain and the ammonia used for cleansing. When the tanks were being cleaned, the bosun nominated one seaman to ensure that the rest of the gang were safely accounted for and had not succumbed to the fumes.

Deck lighting comprised permanent fittings on the underside of the crosstrees, an advance on the usual five-bulb cluster which had to be hauled up the rigging. Alan contrasts working practices with those on the Canadian Pacific 'Beavers' on which he also served on the North Atlantic. In *Alsatia* the guys were stripped from the derricks and stowed under cover instead of being allowed to remain in position and freeze into solid blocks. Another contrast was Cunard's policy of signing on crew for three or four successive voyages, whereas on the 'Beavers' articles had to renewed after every relatively short trip.

In 1963 Cunard sold *Alsatia* and *Andria* to Hong Kong shipowner C.Y. Tung who registered them in Taiwan under the ownership of China Union Lines. *Alsatia* became *Union Freedom* and gave long and useful service in the Far East, not being broken up in Taiwan until 1977.

Although *Alsatia* and *Andria* were replaced with other conventional cargo liners, the intensive and highly competitive cargo services on the North Atlantic were prime targets for containerisation, once the seed of such an idea had been sown in the early 1960s. Cunard naturally joined one of the new container consortia, taking a 25% interest in Atlantic Container Lines. An immediate result of the containerships entering service on the Atlantic was the redundancy of Cunard's conventional freighters, which had gone by 1970, leaving passenger ships as the only users of their celebrated funnel colours.

Alsatia in the English Channel.

Completed in 1948 by J.L. Thompson and Sons Ltd., Sunderland.
7,226 gross tons, 483 feet.
Machinery: three steam turbines by Parsons Marine Steam Turbine Co. Ltd., Wallsend-on-Tyne, geared to a single shaft.

Alsatia off the Ambrose Light Vessel.

ALLY
1955–1958
Eddie Steamship Co. Ltd., Taipei

Eddie Steamship Co. Ltd. was founded in Shanghai in 1927 by industrialist Hsu Ting-cho. Initially its trading area was limited to short routes around Shanghai, the routes to north and south China being the preserve of western powers under what the Chinese referred to as the Unequal Treaties. By 1937 the company had four ships but when the Sino-Japanese War broke out two were requisitioned by the Chinese government, filled with sand and scuttled at the mouth of the Yangtse in an attempt to prevent the Japanese Navy from entering the river.

The end of the Second World War, and the defeat of Japanese forces in China, saw a major improvement in trading opportunities and the Eddie Steamship Company quickly expanded its fleet to five ships, including the *Eddie* depicted here. Under the control of the founder's younger son, W.H. Eddie Hsu, the ships traded more widely, from Shanghai to Taiwan, Tianjin and Guangzhou. But the new-found prosperity was short-lived. As Mao Tse Tung's communists controlled more and more of mainland China, the Hsu family were forced to abandon their business interests in Shanghai, but managed to sail two of their ships to Taiwan and re-establish themselves in the city of Taipei. With the loss of the China coastal trade, the company concentrated on regional trades, to Japan and Korea. During the 1950s, the Korean War and the Suez crisis helped boost demand for shipping, and Eddie Steamship again prospered, expanding its fleet to 15 ships including the *Polly* and *Ally*.

During the 1960s and 1970s the fleet grew to over 50 ships with a total tonnage of 40 million, making it one of the world's largest companies in the bulk trades. With Taiwan's economy growing at 10 per cent annually, trade was booming, and Eddie Steamship prospered. The company carried some 70 per cent of Taiwan's grain imports, 80 per cent of the coal for the state-owned Taiwan Power Company, and 100 per cent of the iron ore for the state steel producer, China Steel. In 1967 the company placed the first of 15 orders for newbuildings in Japan, and in 1970 ordered the first of 16 ships from the fledgling Taiwan Shipbuilding Corporation. The company was one of only two private concerns allowed to invest in the China Shipbuilding Corporation, which built the world's second largest dry dock.

The company was used to crises, but perhaps its worst came in 1984 when, following a prolonged depression in shipping, it faced financial collapse, along with many other shipping companies in the Far East. Although many ships were repossessed by banks, with the help of local Taiwanese banks Eddie Steamship survived and by the time Eddie Hsu died in 1987, had began to rebuild its fleet.

Under managing director Chih-Chien Hsu, Eddie Steamship maintains its business links with Taiwan's state enterprises, and employs a fleet of eight bulk carriers of around 30,000 deadweight, with a couple of Panamax bulkers on charter. In the 1990s it re-opened its historic route from China to Taiwan, and in 1997 carried the first shipment of coal from mainland China to Taiwan, for Taiwan Power.

Eddie Steamship Company has survived three crises to become an important participant in the bulk trade of the Far East.

Polly at Hong Kong

Eddie at Singapore

Ally
Completed 1924 by Napier and Miller Ltd., Glasgow.
5,051 gross tons, 398 feet.
Machinery: triple-expansion steam engine by Napier and Miller Ltd., Glasgow.
Ally was built for a British tramp shipping company as *Framlington Court*, later names being *Stancourt*, *Landscape* and *Ami Banker*. Eddie Steamship bought her at Hong Kong in April 1955. *Ally* was dismantled at Kaohsiung in July 1958.

Ally off Kaohsiung

CITY OF LONDON

1947–1967

Ellerman and Bucknall Steamship Co. Ltd., London

Like all British companies, the Ellerman Group suffered heavily during the Second World War, with losses amongst its owned and managed ships totalling 85. Perhaps the most tragic story began, ominously, on Friday 13th September 1940 when *City of Benares* sailed from Liverpool to Canada as commodore ship of convoy OB213. Among her 406 crew and passengers there were 101 adults and 90 children being evacuated to Canada by the Children's Overseas Reception Board. After just four days, the escort left to accompany an eastbound convoy, leaving *City of Benares* – which was capable of 17 knots – to plod onward at just 8 knots, and unescorted. This was courting disaster, and later that day, at 22.00, the German submarine *U 48* decided that the two-funnelled *City of Benares* made a tempting target. She did not sink immediately following the impact of the torpedo, but conditions in mid-Atlantic made lowering the boats difficult and several capsized. Many of those who did not drown outright died of exposure before the destroyer HMS *Hurricane* arrived the next afternoon. A total of 102 people were rescued, but tragically only seven of them were children. A further boat, initially thought lost, was rescued by HMS *Anthony* on 26th September, but of the 45 on board only six were children. Of *City of Benares*' complement, 245 were lost, including 77 of the children. No wartime losses were easy to bear, but the deaths of their children must have put an intolerable burden on the families who had decided to send them to supposed safety.

With heavy war losses, replacement had to be tackled energetically, and many war-built ships were bought whilst new ships were ordered. The first post-war deliveries were the *City of New York* class, of which *City of London* was the second. They were, essentially, modifications of the pre-war *City of Capetown* design, the changes mercifully including oil rather than coal firing for their steam turbines. Ellerman were not at the forefront of propulsion technology, and at the time of introducing this class the company seem to have had no clear policy on the issue. Indeed, in the year *City of London* was accepted, the Ellerman fleet was taking delivery of ships with steam reciprocating, steam turbine and diesel machinery. As an example of this indecisiveness, the hull of what was to be the fifth member of the *City of New York* class was completed as the

motor ship *City of Johannesburg*, with a rather different profile. Nevertheless, the company continued turning out turbine ships until the mid-1950s.

City of London had her fleeting moment of glory in June 1953, when she represented Ellermans at the Coronation review at Spithead. D.M. Bridge joined her as his second ship as a cadet at Gibraltar in May 1959. He remembers *City of London* as being comfortable but old-fashioned. Her rather aged appearance belied her speed, however, and being capable of 17 knots she surprised many of the ships she overhauled.

Ownership by Ellerman and Bucknall suggests she was intended for South African services; indeed, the class's speed was specified in order that they could reach the Cape from the UK in just 15 days. In practice, *City of London's* service was on whatever Ellerman sailing, be it Bucknall, Hall or City Line, that needed her at the time. One of D.M. Bridge's voyages was typical. After discharging oil drums and some general cargo at Aden, *City of London* proceeded across the Indian Ocean, discharging machinery, chemicals and other general cargo at Bombay, Karachi, Cochin, Madras, Budge Budge, Chittagong and Chalna. After five weeks discharging, she loaded at Calcutta and Vizakhapatam for the USA, proceeding via Suez first to Boston, and then working her way down the coast to complete discharge in Baltimore. At Philadelphia and New York, general cargo and 11 passengers were loaded, and she returned to India. The usual round of discharging was interrupted at Calcutta when *City of London's* starboard propeller struck the support for a road bridge. A new tailshaft had to be sent by air from the UK, and whilst repairs were awaited, her cadets were transferred to the Liberty *City of Ely* to return to the UK.

City of London was sold early in 1967 after almost 20 years of Ellerman service, and became the Greek-owned and flagged *Sandra N*. She was delivered to breakers at Kaohsiung at the very end of 1968.

City of London at the Coronation Review at Spithead. *[F.R. Sherlock]*

Completed in 1947 by Swan, Hunter and Wigham Richardson Ltd., Wallsend-on-Tyne. 8,434 gross tons, 500 feet.
Machinery: six steam turbines by the Wallsend Slipway Co. Ltd., Wallsend-on-Tyne, geared to two shafts.

City of London in the English Channel

DURHAM

1934–1965

Federal Steam Navigation Co. Ltd., London

Durham and her sister Dorset must rank as two of the most celebrated of British cargo liners. They set a style which was to grace the Federal and New Zealand fleets for four decades. The long bridge decks which had been a feature of the fleets for many years gave way to a flush-decked layout. Diesel engines and cargo gear comprising two masts plus kingposts to serve other holds had been pioneered in the Otaio of 1930, and these too were to become trademarks of the group's ships.

Both ships had spectacular war careers during which their participation in some of the most heroic Malta convoys ensured their lasting fame. With their large capacity and speeds of over 16 knots, these twin-screw motorships were natural choices for the convoys. Durham survived her heavily-escorted run to Malta in July 1941, but was not so lucky when making her escape. Her troubles began off Cape Bon, Tunisia on 22nd August when she struck one mine and caught another in her paravane. She reached Gibraltar, but on 18th September was attacked by Italian midget submarines which attached explosive charges to her hull. The extensive damage caused by these, added to that from the mine, meant that Durham did not return to service until late in 1943.

Dorset was less fortunate. In August 1942 during Operation Pedestal, that supreme effort to fight supplies through from Gibraltar to Malta, Dorset lost contact with the convoy after dark on 12th August, and survived mine explosions and an E-boat attack. She rejoined the convoy next day, but a determined air attack during the morning caused damage and fires, which threatened to ignite the aviation spirit on board and she had to be abandoned. Although only five of the 14 merchant ships which set out from Gibraltar reached Malta, the cargoes that did get through helped the island play a decisive role in the eventual victory in North Africa.

In 1955 Durham resumed her role as a cadet ship after a refit at Falmouth. The 34 cadets were accommodated in three-berth cabins built within the 'tween deck of number six hold. Apart from two able seamen, the cadets did all the deck work, from blacking down the standing rigging and running gear, chipping rust and painting the ship – which was completed from top to waterline every trip. The cadets were divided into three groups: seniors, intermediates and juniors, each group having a school session in the well-appointed classroom

every morning, afternoon or evening. The cadets also supplied the watch keepers – at sea these were the helmsman and lookout, and in port the gangway watch.

The responsibilities given to cadets could be considerable. As a Durham cadet, Glen Smith was helmsman during her first transit of the Suez Canal after its closure following the Suez War in 1956. The pilot gave him helm orders which he repeated and carried out exactly. The pilot's orders had the ship swinging from port to starboard and back again, each time with increased amplitude. When the Durham was in the centre of the canal the pilot merely said 'midships', which did nothing to stop the swing. Inevitably, the ship ended up outside the buoyed channel, stopping abruptly with a list to starboard. Luckily, the main damage was to the lunch, which ended up on the galley floor as the cooks had not fitted the dodgers which were usually fixed to the stoves at sea.

Durham carried two whalers on the forward boat deck, and the cadets prided themselves on their rowing ability. In his three years on Durham, Glen recalls that they never lost a race, which took place over a one-mile course. He remembers beating the flagships of the Australian and New Zealand Navies, and of the Royal Navy's Mediterranean Fleet. The nearest they came to a defeat was at the hands of Pitcairn Islanders, whose boat was crewed entirely by men named Fletcher or Christian. The Durham lads won because they were younger and fitter. Perhaps this was due to the ship carrying an ex-services physical training instructor, who took the cadets for PT at 6.30 every morning.

Glen Smith looks back on his time in Durham with affection and notes that many of her cadets finished up with interesting and responsible jobs. At one time no fewer than 21 of the Federal and New Zealand companies' ships were commanded by men who had been cadets on Durham.

Durham's career ended in 1965, but the old lady had only to suffer the indignity of a flag-of-convenience for one voyage to Kaohsiung where she arrived for demolition in March 1966 under the name Rion.

Preliminary sketch for the painting of Durham.

Completed in 1934 by Workman, Clark (1928) Ltd., Belfast.
10,624 gross tons, 494 feet.
Machinery: 16-cylinder oil engine by Workman, Clark (1928) Ltd., Belfast.

Durham entering the Royal Docks, London

BAVARIA
1966–1986

BREMEN
1957–1972

Hapag-Lloyd A.G., Bremen

With the 21-knot *Bavaria* and her six sisters, Hamburg-Amerika Linie were responding to the same pressures to reduce voyage times to the Far East as were other liner companies including Ben, Blue Funnel and Glen. And like the British ships, they were quickly displaced from their intended routes by container ships.

Running on routes which were not yet fully containerised, several of the class were used as training ships. Karl-Heinz Hilbig began his sea-going career in 1973 as a cadet with Hapag-Lloyd A.G., formed when Hamburg-Amerika merged with Bremen-based Norddeutscher Lloyd in September 1970. In addition to the standard crew on *Bavaria*, there were 11 cadets. The one-time passenger cabins were used for their accommodation and class rooms. From Monday to Friday there were lessons each morning, whilst in the afternoons the cadets worked on deck supervised by the training bosun. Saturday morning was spent on cleaning jobs, and Saturday afternoon and Sunday were spent studying.

Karl-Heinz's first voyage took him from Bremerhaven, via Amsterdam and other European ports, round the Cape of Good Hope to Indonesia, including several ports in Sumatra, Java and the Celebes where general cargo from Europe was discharged using when necessary the 80-ton Stülcken derrick. Cargo carried outward included tobacco, timber, rattan and frozen seafood. The *Bavaria* had tanks on the after deck which were used to carry general cargo from Europe for the first discharge port. Then a team of 30 local tank cleaners came on board and sailed with the vessel, being accommodated under the forecastle (dubbed 'Hotel Indonesia'), and in containers on deck, and having their own kitchen. This team cleaned and coated the tanks in readiness for loading liquids such as latex and palm oil.

Six months was spent as a cadet, approximating to two round voyages in these fast ships. There was then an examination, and the successful cadets became apprentices, distributed over the Hapag-Lloyd fleet, with one or two on each cargo ship. In the 1970s, twelve months as an apprentice was followed by at least three years at nautical college.

In 1979, the *Bavaria* was transferred to a subsidiary company, Hapag-Lloyd International S.A. of Panama, although she remained under the German flag with Hamburg as her port of registry. German companies were skilled at finding employment for ships and crews under other flags and ownership. Karl-Heinz recalls that he was Second Officer in 1981 on one of *Bavaria's* sisters, the *Alemannia*. She had been sold two years earlier to Lineas Navieras Bolivianas of La Paz, but still carried officers from Hapag-Lloyd, with cadets and ratings from Bolivia. At one time the *Alemannia* received a visit from a Bolivian admiral: the total lack of a coast line did not inhibit the country's naval ambitions.

Bavaria was broken up in Taiwan, arriving at Kaohsiung in December 1986.

Bremen, seen in the background, was bought by Norddeutscher Lloyd in 1957 to help re-open their North Atlantic passenger services. She was built as *Pasteur* of Compagnie de Navigation Sudatlantique of Bordeaux, the fastest French ship for the South Atlantic trade, and another of the great passenger liners from the 1930s whose destiny was shaped by war. *Pasteur* was due to sail on her maiden voyage to South America in September 1939 but when war was declared her owners decided to lay her up at Saint Nazaire. When the fall of France was imminent in June 1940, her passenger

fittings were hurriedly stripped out and, after loading France's gold reserves, *Pasteur* dashed across the North Atlantic to Canada. She was at sea when France capitulated and whilst in Halifax was requisitioned by the British government as a troopship, and is reckoned to have carried some 300,000 personnel during the war. *Pasteur* was returned to France in June 1945, but continued life as a troopship, mainly running to Indo-China where France was fighting to retain her colonies.

Needing almost complete rebuilding when bought in 1957, the ship was sent to Bremer Vulkan's yard at Vegesack. Some 18 months of work was required, the bill for which is said to have been the equivalent of £6 million, three times her purchase price. The refit included a new funnel, much improving her appearance. Renamed *Bremen* she made her maiden voyage on her new route from Bremerhaven via Cherbourg and Southampton to New York in July 1959.

Karl-Heinz Hilbig reports that, initially at least, *Bremen* was very popular. This was not just with passengers, as her calls at the passenger terminal at Columbuskaje, Bremerhaven were often witnessed by thousands of visitors, although some were welcoming home the many crew members who lived in the port. The *Bremen* was also renowned for the excellent 'Lloydservice' on board.

In the late sixties, however, problems were mounting. Competition from airlines grew, the exchange rate made German ships expensive to sail on, and *Bremen* was not cheap to run with her large crew, compounded by growing problems with her machinery which needed many extra engineers. Although bookings for sailings in 1970 stood at an impressive 85% of capacity, Hapag-Lloyd (as her owners had become) decided to quit the North Atlantic route, and in October 1971 *Bremen* was sold to the Chandris group, who renamed her *Regina Magna* in 1972 and sent her cruising.

But the old ship was too large and expensive to succeed in the cruise market, and after just two years she was laid up at Piraeus. This would normally signal the end of a ship's working life, but her hull was reprieved in 1977 when she was sent to Jeddah for use as an accommodation ship for the thousands of Philippine stevedores working in the port. Initially renamed *Saudiphil I*, she later became *Saudi Filipinas I*. Sold for scrapping in 1980, she managed to cheat the breakers. Whilst under tow for Taiwan, she developed a list and sank in the Arabian Sea on 9th June 1980. Perhaps it could be considered a dignified death for a ship which over 40 years had four careers under five national flags.

Bavaria
Completed in 1966 by Blohm und Voss A.G., Hamburg.
10,915 gross tons, 540 feet.
Machinery: nine-cylinder MAN-type oil engines by Blohm und Voss A.G., Hamburg.

Bremen
Completed in 1939 by Chantiers et Ateliers de St. Nazaire S.A. (Penhoët), St. Nazaire.
32,336 gross tons, 673 feet.
Machinery: four Parsons-type steam turbines by Chantiers et Ateliers de St. Nazaire S.A. (Penhoët), St. Nazaire, driving four shafts.

Bavaria and *Bremen* passing Rotesand after leaving Bremerhaven

FACTOR
1948–1972
The Charente Steamship Co. Ltd. (T. and J. Harrison Ltd., managers), Liverpool

Harrison Line was a particularly conservative organisation, one of the last British liner companies to adopt the diesel engine. A class of three ships, the *Herdsman* of 1947, the *Interpreter* and the *Factor* of 1948 were the company's first motor ships. But there were obviously still doubts about this method of propulsion as, contemporary with their delivery, a class of traditional steam-reciprocating-engined vessels were also being added to the fleet, the *Craftsman* (illustrated in 'The British Merchant Navy: Images and Experiences'), *Linguist* and *Biographer*. In many ways these were similar to the pre-war ships of the Inventor type, one of which is portrayed in the accompanying sketch. Not surprisingly, the diesel won and subsequent Harrison ships were so equipped.

It often happens that ships nominally of the same class behave very differently, and this was true of the *Factor* and sisters. *Factor* was a rather different ship to handle. George Nicholson, *Factor's* First Officer during the 1950s, remembers her as being more sea kindly than *Interpreter*, which he remembers as rolling all the way across the Atlantic to Galveston during his first voyage as a cadet. He attributed *Factor's* better performance and slightly better speed to her having a slightly narrower beam, but being built on the Clyde may also have made a difference.

There were also significant differences in the experiences of the ships of this class. *Factor* led an almost completely blameless life, and the only occasion she was in major trouble seems to have been due to natural causes, rather than to human error. On 26th July 1951, she twice grounded heavily on the Magdalena Bar in the approach to Boca Ceniza in Colombia. Such was the damage that she was making water in three holds. All her cargo was discharged at Barranquilla where temporary repairs were made so that she could sail to the nearest available dry dock, in Galveston. Examination revealed extensive damage, with a total of 48 plates needing repair or replacement, and eight tank tops needing to be renewed. As was their wont, Harrison Line carried out a searching enquiry about the accident, and would have been most intolerant of any misdemeanour by master or officers. In the event, no satisfactory cause could be found for the grounding, and the most likely explanation was that a minor earthquake, for which the area was known,

had distorted the sea bed in the vicinity. *Factor's* master, Captain William H. Allen, was completely exonerated. He had joined Harrisons way back in 1934 when they acquired a group of ships from Leyland Line, but not being 'home grown' he had to wait until he was 58 for promotion to master. He retired at the end of the year of the Magdalena Bar incident, aged 65.

In contrast to *Factor*, *Interpreter* was rarely out of trouble. When he heard of *Interpreter's* second serious grounding within the space of seven months, a senior superintendent in Harrison Line commented that 'they should have given that ship wheels'. The first of her mishaps occurred when leaving St. John's Harbour, Antigua in June 1955 when she ran hard on to a coral reef. Transferring some of her cargo to another ship allowed *Interpreter* to be quickly refloated, but it was too late to save her master's career with the company. The ship was ordered to remain in Antigua, and another senior master was flown out to relieve him, and the *Interpreter's* captain took passage home to the inevitable enquiry which was likely to lead to his dismissal. *Interpreter's* next master fared no better. He was in command in January 1956 when, approaching the channel to the Texas port of Corpus Christi, the ship ran onto a sandy beach at a full 14 knots. Conditions were difficult: visibility was bad, thundery conditions frustrated attempts to use her radio direction finder, and her echo sounder was not functioning. But all this counted for nought in her master's defence. Although spared the indignity of being almost instantly relieved of his command, there could only be one result of the enquiry when *Interpreter* returned to Liverpool for repairs. After 38 years' service, including the hazards of the Second World War, a man with an otherwise exemplary record was summarily dismissed from Harrison's service. Today it seems to us surprising that Harrison's officers showed so much loyalty to such a hard and unforgiving company.

After a career of 24 years, *Factor* was sold to breakers during March 1972 and demolished at Bilbao.

Factor
Completed in 1948 by Charles Connell and Co. Ltd., Scotstoun.
6,533 gross tons, 464 feet.
Machinery: Doxford-type five-cylinder oil engine by Barclay, Curle and Co. Ltd., Glasgow.

An Inventor class ship enters Liverpool Docks

Factor in the Mersey

RATHLIN HEAD

1953–1970

The Ulster Steamship Co. Ltd. (G. Heyn and Sons Ltd., managers), Belfast

Although the home of one of the world's most celebrated shipbuilders, the city of Belfast is not so well known for its shipowners. The most successful, and the longest lived, was the Heyn family, who cemented their connection with Ireland by naming many of their ships after headlands around the coast. Not surprisingly, their fleet came to be known as the Head Line.

As the name Heyn suggests, the founder of the company was not Irish by birth, but from Danzig, then part of Prussia. Fortuitously, when Gustavus Heyn arrived in Belfast as Consul for Prussia in 1825, he lodged with a William Pirrie. Marrying Pirrie's daughter Letitia was to give the Heyns an important connection with a later and more famous William Pirrie: the Lord Pirrie who was such an influential chairman of Harland and Wolff Ltd. who were to build many Head Line ships.

Gustavus Heyn and his sons began in business as shipbrokers and merchants, then followed the familiar path into shipowning. The Ulster Steamship Co. Ltd., incorporated in 1877, initially operated services to Russian ports in the Baltic, but later became better known for its trade to the eastern seaboard of North America. Heyns were also involved in liner services from Ireland to continental Europe, Irish livestock being a speciality.

Rathlin Head was one of a class of three steam-turbine-driven cargo liners ordered after the Second World War. She was actually completed some 24 feet shorter than her near sisters, *Roonagh Head* and *Ramore Head*, so that she could use Waterford Harbour.

The task of standing by these new post-war ships fell to Head Line's commodore, Captain Erele Wilmot Black, who was one of those remarkable officers who began his career as an ordinary seaman. His first ship was the *Torr Head* in 1912, and in June 1917 he survived the torpedoing of *Bengore Head*. Immediately after the war he began studying for his officer's certificates, but it was not until 1935 that he got his first full-time command, the *Orlock Head*. Captain Black established his reputation as a seaman on the *Torr Head* when her rudder post fractured in the North

Atlantic during the Second World War. The rudder was at an angle at the time, and to allow the ship to be steered an attempt was made to attach wires to the rudder, but this proved impossible from a small workboat in Atlantic swells. Eventually, a drag was streamed over the stern to counteract the effect of the rudder and, with no assistance or escort, *Torr Head* was brought slowly into Sydney, Cape Breton. In recognition of this achievement, Captain Black received an OBE in 1944. His appointment as Commodore of Head Line followed. Although it became more difficult when cadetships and apprenticeships were widely instituted, it was a feature of the Merchant Navy that a man who began as a humble seaman could, with perseverance, rise right through the ranks, as Captain Black so ably demonstrated. He retired in 1960.

The opening of the St. Lawrence Seaway in 1960 saw Head Line concentrating on services to Canada and the Great Lakes. In common with other companies trading to this area, the line's name was painted prominently on the ships' sides. This trade was buoyant for a few years but towards the end of the 1960s container ships began to claim much of the cargo. In a brave attempt to contend with much richer rivals, Head joined with the Glasgow-based Donaldson Line to operate a joint service, and in 1970 converted the conventional cargo vessel *Inishowen Head* to a container ship. But the Head-Donaldson service could not compete with operators of much larger, purpose-built container ships. From 1970, when *Rathlin Head* was sold, the fleet was quickly run down, the *Inishowen Head* being chartered out to erstwhile rivals in 1973. The Heyn Group, as it became, remained active in providing services to shipping in Belfast.

On her sale in 1970 the *Rathlin Head* went to Greek owners and was registered in Cyprus as the *George*. She lasted until August 1972 when a Spanish shipbreaker began to dismantle her.

Completed in 1953 by Harland and Wolff Ltd., Belfast.
7,378 gross tons, 406 feet.
Machinery: two steam turbines by Harland and Wolff Ltd., Belfast, double-reduction geared to a single shaft.

Rathlin Head in the Mersey. [*Basil Feilden*]

Rathlin Head

NIEUW AMSTERDAM
1938–1974

VOLENDAM
1922–1952

Holland-Amerika Lijn, Rotterdam

Nieuw Amsterdam was a ship that inspired enormous affection, and not only amongst the Dutch for whom she was a national flagship for many years. She came from a classic era, becoming one of the last operational ships from the golden age of the transatlantic liner.

Ordering the ship in the 1930s was something of an act of faith, as times were hard and Holland-Amerika's existing passenger ships were not prospering. With other maritime nations - UK, Germany, France and Italy – commissioning impressive, and usually state-subsidised, transatlantic passenger ships, the Dutch simply had to follow suit to stay in the game.

By all accounts, the Nieuw Amsterdam created a striking impression in those who inspected her. A technical journal wrote that she presented 'an imposing, not to say exhilarating spectacle'. Naval architect Stephen Payne, who has designed major liners himself, wrote that 'the shapely curve of the stem and cruiser stern, lofty superstructure, two streamlined funnels and tall masts, combined with a grace of line, gave the ship an altogether magnificent aspect'. Accommodation was described as 'creating an atmosphere of refined comfort rather than ostentatious luxury'. The first class dining area and the Grand Hall were particularly notable, extending vertically through two decks and being lavishly decorated and beautifully lit. Nieuw Amsterdam performed as well as she looked. Naval architect Sir William Isherwood was on her maiden voyage in July 1938, and reported that 'she's as safe and strong as a ship can be. We had a bit of a pitching sea the second day out, and last night a rolling sea. But she rode well and is a very, very steady ship'.

The outbreak of the Second World War meant that the Nieuw Amsterdam had little more than a year in transatlantic service before being laid up for safety at the Hoboken piers in New York. She did make a number of cruises to the West Indies, and during one of these her crew learnt that the Netherlands had been invaded. The ship was offered to the British government, and taken to the relative safety of Singapore. Here all her luxurious fittings were summarily stripped out in readiness for her use as a troopship, in which role she could accommodate 8,000 personnel. There are no reports of untoward incidents during her six years of trooping.

Return to her owners and home port of Rotterdam in April 1946 saw Nieuw Amsterdam go back to her builder's yard for a refit. As her original

fittings had been hastily removed and mostly been stored as far away as Singapore and Sydney, the work was extensive and took 14 months. It included sanding down the teak decking and hand rails on which bored troops had carved their initials.

The post-war years were successful ones for Nieuw Amsterdam. Periodic refits maintained her standards, and included repainting from black to grey in 1957 and air conditioning of her cabins and stabilisers installed in 1961.

Mechanical troubles became apparent in 1967, when some of her boilers began to fail. The owners' dilemma over whether to fit expensive replacements to a ship which was now 29 years old was solved by purchasing five boilers designed for wartime US cruisers, most of which had hardly been used. It was reported that Nieuw Amsterdam steamed better than ever after this.

Holland-Amerika abandoned transatlantic passenger sailings in September 1971, and Nieuw Amsterdam went cruising. However, in only two years her owners were having severe financial problems, with rising fuel and crewing costs, and expensive purchases of new and used ships. With her high fuel consumption and large crew, Nieuw Amsterdam had to go, even though she was considered sound enough for several more years' service, and she was broken up at Kaohsiung. She had performed as well as she had looked during her 36-year career.

The painting opposite depicts Volendam, one of Nieuw Amsterdam's forerunners, around 1930 when the River Maas was frozen and the steam tugs of the Port of Rotterdam 'Havendienst' with their limited power had problems getting through the ice. The view is looking east, towards the Maasbruggen. Volendam survived the war and was broken up in Holland during 1952.

Nieuw Amsterdam at New York, also reproduced on the dust jacket

Nieuw Amsterdam
Completed in 1938 by N.V. Rotterdam Droogdok Maatschappij, Rotterdam.
36,287 gross tons, 758 feet.
Machinery: eight steam turbines by Koninklijke Maatschappij 'De Schelde', Vlissingen single-reduction geared to twin screws.

Volendam
Completed in 1922 by Harland and Wolff Ltd., Glasgow.
15,434 gross tons, 550 feet.
Machinery: four steam turbines by Harland and Wolff Ltd., Belfast, single-reduction geared to two shafts.

Volendam leaving the Holland-Amerika terminal at Rotterdam

LADY OF MANN

1976–

Isle of Man Steam Packet Co. Ltd., Douglas

The Isle of Man Steam Packet Co. Ltd. has a long and proud history, with a fair claim to being one of the oldest surviving shipping companies. Founded in 1830 and adopting its present name two years later, the company was seven years old at the birth of P&O, and only Bibby has a claim to greater longevity. Recent years have not been the company's most glorious, and ownership has passed outside the Isle of Man, but after 175 years it is still operating across the same stretch of water, the Irish Sea.

Steamer services from Liverpool to Douglas began in 1819, but the island was served largely by packets running between the Mersey and the Clyde. With their own strong seafaring traditions, the independently-minded Manx wanted their own steamers, and a public meeting in Douglas led to the formation of the Mona's Isle Company, whose first paddle steamer was naturally named *Mona's Isle*. The present name was adopted in 1832.

Over the years, the company's business has changed, as indeed has the nature of the Isle of Man's business. At the foundation of the company, the island economy was based largely on agriculture and seafaring. In the late 19th century, tourism began to grow, and the fleet expanded accordingly. The author of these captions made several crossings for family holidays in the 1950s, at the time the fleet was at its peak. Two survivors from the pre-war fleet, *Lady of Mann* (1) and *Ben-my-Chree* (4), had been joined by six turbine steamers built post-war, and there were two steam and one motor coaster. In the summer, all eight conventional passenger steamers were fully employed running to Douglas, on routes not just from Liverpool, but also from Heysham, Ardrossan, Belfast and Dublin. On August Saturdays their capacity to carry 2,000 passengers was used to the full, but in the winter all but a few went into lay-up.

The ships were very conventional. Passengers were rigidly segregated by class, with second class aft. As a teenager the author remembers being frustrated that the only time he could look 'ahead' on *Ben-my-Chree* was when backing out of Douglas harbour. Steam turbines continued to be specified and holidaymakers wanting to take their cars to the island had to watch them being craned on and off.

Vehicle ferries came very late to the Isle of Man, and the parsimony of authorities on both sides of the Irish Sea limited the service to cars. The first car ferry, the steam-turbine driven *Manx Maid* of 1962, was a side loader, as neither Liverpool nor Douglas would contemplate the expense of a linkspan to offer proper ro-ro facilities. This precluded use of the ferry by freight vehicles.

The second *Lady of Mann* was the fourth car ferry, and the only radical difference from the pioneer *Manx Maid* built 14 years earlier were her diesel engines. Her name was an auspicious one, as the only previous occasion it had been used was on a ship built to celebrate the company's centenary in 1930. This *Lady of Mann* was the largest ship yet built for the company, and with her speed, good looks, seaworthiness and spacious decks was a worthy flagship for a remarkable 42 years.

When the second *Lady of Mann* was built, Manx tourism was in decline, and the fleet was being purged of its conventional steamers. To add to the Steam Packet's woes, rival services began using 'proper' ro-ro ships, and, although they were initially badly run, they encouraged major operators to take an interest in the Steam Packet's monopoly. To compete, better ships and hence more money were needed, and in raising extra finance the company has drifted out of Manx ownership. There must be doubts about the wisdom of the Manx government, a major shareholder, losing control of the island's major lifeline. This is especially so as the island's economy has boomed in recent years as its benevolent tax regime attracted much business, including – ironically – ship management.

But the *Lady of Mann* soldiered on, latterly on charter in Portuguese waters. Although a long way off the age achieved by the previous *Lady of Mann*, almost 30 years in the same ownership is a good record, especially for a ship which even when new was something of an anachronism.

Lady of Mann (2)
Completed in 1976 by the Ailsa Shipbuilding Co. Ltd., Troon.
2,990 gross tons, 104.4 metres.
Machinery: two Pielstick-type 12-cylinder oil engines by Crossley-Premier Engines Ltd., Manchester.

The first *Lady of Mann*, the company's centenary ship, approaches Douglas. *[Basil Feilden]*

Lady of Mann sails from Douglas

ANDREA DORIA
1953–1956
'Italia' Societa per Azioni di Navigazione, Genoa

When *Andrea Doria* was completed, Italia Line's publicity department waxed lyrical about the largest and fastest Italian-built liner since the Second World War. 'The new liner was designed and built by great naval architects, manned by seamen of Genoese stock. The ship has been decorated with loving care and delicate taste by the best artists of Italy who combined modern luxury and comfort with graceful old world beauty. Spacious accommodation provided room for 1,200 passengers in three classes, all bound to enjoy the advantages of the mild climate of the sunny southern route to Europe, all ready to exploit the freedom of three lido decks, each with its own tiled swimming pool. The *Andrea Doria* is the first ship to be completely air conditioned throughout from passenger staterooms and public rooms to service areas and crew quarters.'

'More than two score artists, architects and designers embellished the 31 public rooms on the *Andrea Doria* with Italy's best painters, sculptors and wood carvers contributing to make the 30,000 ton flagship of the Italian Merchant Marine a floating gallery of art. From the 'Legend of Italy', a large painting reproducing Italian art masterpieces in the First Class Lounge, to the murals representing farm activities in the Tourist Class Dining Room, art is a part of everyday life onboard.'

'The *Andrea Doria* epitomizes the Italian heritage in the fine arts. Rare and costly woods, novel lighting, specially-designed and woven fabrics . . . new concepts of comfort and beauty are harmoniously blended to make a great ship. A spirit of gracious living animates her, expressed in traditionally fine hospitality, service and superb cuisine. Into the careful planning of the *Andrea Doria* have gone years of Italian Line experience in pleasing exacting tastes'.

'And the perfect finishing touch to make a crossing to Europe on the Sunny Southern Route a truly memorable travel experience? Why, of course it's the traditionally fine Italian Line service. You'll find your every need catered to, almost before you think of it. You'll delight in the superb continental cuisine.' Travellers from the USA would believe they were already in Europe once they stepped aboard.

The new liner entered service with a shake-down cruise over the Christmas and New Years holidays in December 1952 and commenced her maiden voyage from Genoa to New York via Cannes, Naples and Gibraltar on 14th January 1953. She received a big welcome upon arriving in New York in the early morning of 23rd January. But she was not to remain the Italia Line's flagship for long; the similar but slightly larger *Cristoforo Colombo* took the title when she entered service in July 1954.

Andrea Doria was to achieve lasting fame, not for being 'a floating gallery of art' nor for her continental cuisine, but for becoming one of the most serious post-war casualties amongst passenger vessels. The 'great naval architects' who designed her must bear some of the blame for the tragedy.

Just after midnight on 25th July 1956 she was inward bound for New York and steaming through dense fog near Nantucket Island when she was hit below the navigating bridge by the Swedish liner *Stockholm*, herself outward bound from New York. The *Andrea Doria's* hull was divided into 11 watertight compartments, and it was claimed that any two could be flooded without affecting her stability. Although *Stockholm* pierced only one compartment, *Andrea Doria* at once took a heavy list, which increased until water was pouring in through cabin port holes.

The heavy list made launching her lifeboats very difficult, although some managed to get away. Fortunately, *Andrea Doria* remained afloat for ten hours, and in this time four other ships, including US Navy craft and the French Line's *Ile de France*, came to offer assistance and took off the bulk of her passengers. Although herself badly damaged, *Stockholm* took off over 500 passengers before heading back to New York. This assistance reduced the death toll to 47 passengers and crew on the *Andrea Doria*, and five members of the crew of *Stockholm*.

Sketch for the painting of *Andrea Doria*.

Completed in 1956 by S.A. Ansaldo, Genoa-Sestri.
29,083 gross tons, 700 feet.
Machinery: six steam turbines by S.A. Ansaldo, Genoa-Sampierdarena, single-reduction geared to two shafts.

Andrea Doria off Cape Spartivento, Sardinia

VOLTAIRE

1923–1941

Lamport and Holt Ltd., Liverpool

The 'Vs', represented here by the second *Voltaire*, were the most splendid collection of liners Lamport and Holt owned during their long history. In 1898 the company's occasional voyage from Buenos Aires to New York developed into a regular service calling at Montevideo, Santos and Rio de Janeiro, carrying passengers, live cattle and coffee. This proved to be such a success that larger ships were needed. So out came the first of the 'Vs', the *Veronese* from Belfast in January 1906, and the *Velasquez* from Middlesbrough in February 1906. The same year two more were ordered, the first *Voltaire* from the Clyde, and from Belfast the somewhat smaller *Verdi*. Of the 'Vs', the *Verdi* was the only ship not used on the Buenos Aires to New York route, spending the whole of her career on the Liverpool to Buenos Aires service. In 1908 the *Vasari* was ordered, of a similar length to *Voltaire* and the first of the group to be propelled by quadruple-expansion engines.

In 1910 further 'Vs' were ordered, all from Workman, Clark: the sisters *Vandyck*, *Vauban* and *Vestris*, larger again than the *Vasari*, and all driven by quadruple-expansion engines. However, before they were completed control of the company had passed to Lamport and Holt's rivals on South American routes, the Royal Mail Steam Packet Company, and Owen Cosby Phillipps, later Lord Kylsant, had become chairman. In spite of this, the two companies continued to operate as separate entities.

Following the First World War, new ships were needed, and orders were placed with Workman, Clark for two larger vessels which took the names of two of their predecessors which had been sunk by enemy raiders during hostilities, *Vandyck* and *Voltaire*. The first to be launched, in February 1921, was *Vandyck*, a twin-screw ship driven by steam turbines. At the time of *Vandyck*'s launch, her sister ship, *Voltaire*, had been expected to take the water in April or May, but the completion and the launch of the respective sisters were both delayed because *Vandyck*'s turbines suffered excessive vibration. It was decided to give the *Voltaire* quadruple-expansion engines and this considerably delayed her completion. The three pre-war 'V's shared service with them.

But this all ended with the tragic loss of the *Vestris* in 1928 whilst on a voyage from London and New York for Buenos Aires, with 129 passengers and a crew of 150. On the morning of 12th November an SOS was received from

her, in position some 400 miles off Hampton Roads, saying that she was sinking, with all passengers and crew taking to the lifeboats in heavy seas. Before a rescue ship could arrive, some of the boats were overwhelmed and 112 lives were lost.

The loss of the *Vestris* followed that of an Italian liner off the Brazilian coast the previous year. Together, these losses led to the New York to Buenos Aires service collapsing. The two older 'V's were laid up and eventually sold.

Lamport and Holt was left with two splendid ships which it seemed entirely uncertain how to employ, and until late 1932 *Voltaire* and *Vandyck* were laid up off Netley in Southampton Water. Eventually, the growing popularity of cruising prompted the company to use them for Mediterranean cruises. So, late in 1932, the two sisters were handed over to Harland and Wolff, who completely refurbished them. This included giving them white hulls, a distinctive feature of cruising liners of that time. From 1933 until the outbreak of war in 1939 the sisters spent the summers cruising and the winters laid up.

When war was declared in 1939, the sisters were just finishing their cruising for the year and the Admiralty quickly took them up for conversion to armed merchant cruisers, a course of action which had proved so successful between 1914 and 1918. However, neither ship proved adequate for this type of work, probably because they were too small.

After trooping to Bombay, *Voltaire* was briefly sent to Scapa Flow, but was then fully armed as a convoy escort. She spent most of 1940 as an inspection ship in the Mediterranean, but was then based at Freetown in Sierra Leone to escort convoys across the Atlantic to Halifax. Returning from one of these trips she was attacked by the German commerce raider *Thor* on 9th April 1941. After a fight that lasted nearly two hours the last of the 'V's in Lamport and Holt service was abandoned in sinking condition. Out of her complement of 272 men, 75 were killed and the remainder taken prisoner.

Voltaire. [Basil Feilden]

Completed in 1923 by Workman, Clark and Co. Ltd., Belfast.
13,248 gross tons, 511 feet.
Machinery: two quadruple-expansion four-cylinder steam engines by Workman, Clark and Co. Ltd., Belfast, driving twin shafts.

Voltaire as a cruise ship in the River Mersey

SYLVIA LYKES

1947–1970

Lykes Brothers Steamship Co. Inc., New Orleans

Lykes Lines enjoyed a rather rapid rise to prominence in the early 20th century, but then had an equally rapid fall from grace in the last years of this century. No fewer than seven of the Lykes brothers were involved in the early years, when the company was chartering ships to carry cattle and other commodities from the southern United States and Central America to Cuba. By 1922 the business was expanding, acquiring ships built for the United States government during the First World War – a story which was to be repeated after the next war. Lykes Brothers Steamship Co. Inc. made some monumental acquisitions of other lines, including no fewer than 52 ships from the Dixie and Southern State Lines during the 1930s. By then, they had expanded to operate services to north Europe and to the Mediterranean.

In 1936 the US government, keen to rejuvenate the country's merchant fleet as international tension grew, began a modest programme of shipbuilding, a programme which was to be massively expanded as the situation deteriorated into war. Lykes were to take 28 of these new ships, but as the US was engulfed in the Second World War most new ships were placed under government ownership, although Lykes managed many. Although the owned fleet reached 47 ships in 1947, a massive total of 98 were on charter. The company began expanding its fleet rapidly when war-built ships began to be released to private owners, Sylvia Lykes being bought in 1947, having been completed in May 1945 as the C2-type Asterion.

The C2 was an early design of the United States Maritime Commission which had been set up pre-war to help with the reconstruction of the US merchant fleet. The C2s were fast, turbine-driven 'tween deck steamers, intended for cargo liner operations but with the intention of being useful to the military. Thus they had a reserve of power over that required to maintain a service speed of 15 knots. Appropriately in view of their speed, the earliest C2s

completed in 1939 were given some of the romantic names once applied to the US clippers of the 1840s and 1850s, including *Lightning*, *Sea Witch*, *Flying Cloud*, and *Red Jacket*.

In post war years Lykes Brothers was an important force in shipping, serving especially New Orleans and the southern states. However, as with all US lines, the country's economic strength made life difficult. Protectionist laws meant that ships wearing the US flag had to be built in US yards and manned by US subjects. But both shipbuilding and manning costs in the USA were much higher than elsewhere. As the fleet of mostly C2-types represented by *Sylvia Lykes* and her sisters was retired (she was broken up at Kaohsiung in July 1970), replacements could only be afforded with a government subsidy. However, some fine ships were built, and the lives of some extended, so that Lykes were operating some of the last steam-turbine powered cargo liners. A bold move was into the 'lighter aboard ship' concept, in which ships carried barges which at terminal ports were floated out of the hull and towed to their destination along small waterways. This concept suited the area of Lykes' home

Sylvia Lykes.

operations around the Mississippi Delta, and found some take-up in north European ports with extensive waterway connections, but its success was limited. After indifferent trading results, Lykes Brothers were forced to file for protection from its creditors in 1995. In 1997 came the final ignominy for a once huge and proud fleet, sale to become a subsidiary of Canadian Pacific, now the largest carrier on the North Atlantic.

Completed in 1945 by the Moore Dry Dock Company, Oakland, California. 6,214 gross tons, 439 feet. Machinery: two steam turbines by the General Electric Company, Lynn, Massachusetts geared to one shaft.

Sylvia Lykes passing the Ambrose Light

RANGITATA

1929–1962

New Zealand Shipping Co. Ltd., London

The three passenger ships which the New Zealand Shipping Co. Ltd. built in the late 1920s were amongst the first of their type fitted with diesels, but the motor ship fashion for stumpy funnels robbed them of a truly impressive appearance. These twin-screw ships were notable not only for being the first of the New Zealand company's ships with oil engines, but also because their Brown-Sulzer diesels had the largest output per cylinder then achieved.

Construction of the first, *Rangitiki*, was spread over three years, such was the uncertainty of trading conditions. But she and her sisters, *Rangitata* and *Rangitane*, must have been some of the best investments the company made, with two having careers of well over 30 years. For passenger ships to serve just one owner for over three decades was impressive.

Rangitiki's war service as a trooper was outstanding, although in November 1940 she and much of her convoy were saved only by the self-sacrifice of the *Jervis Bay* in taking on the German pocket-battleship *Admiral Scheer*.

The third of the company's passenger ships, the *Rangitane*, became one of the largest, and certainly the most valuable, victims of German auxiliary cruisers when she fell in with the *Komet* and *Orion* north of New Zealand on 26th November 1940. Masquerading as Japanese neutrals, the German auxiliaries' attack was savage, probably in reprisal for the *Rangitane*'s continuing to send radio messages. There were 13 casualties amongst passengers and crew before the firing stopped and the motor liner was evacuated and sunk by torpedo. Of the 299 survivors from *Rangitane*, 90 were taken back to internment in Germany, whilst the rest were put ashore in the Solomon Islands, later being rescued and taken to Australia.

After the war both *Rangitata* and *Rangitiki* were re-engined as part of a rebuilding which reduced passenger accommodation from 600 in three classes to around 400 in two. They continued to run, from 1949 with the new *Rangitoto* and a second *Rangitane*, and from 1951 with the smaller *Ruahine*, on what the crews proudly pointed out was the longest open sea route on earth, 12,000 miles from London to Wellington, New Zealand via Curacao for bunkers, the Panama Canal, and Tahiti. After passengers disembarked at Wellington, the ships

might visit Auckland, and ports such as Lyttelton and Timaru in South Island before returning to Wellington to complete loading and embark passengers. On the homeward voyage, the itinerary was varied with calls at Kingston, Jamaica, at Miami and Hamilton, Bermuda. Passengers and mail were usually disembarked at Southampton.

When setting out from London, the engineers would note down the readings on the engine revolution counter, and amuse themselves by placing bets on what the reading would be when 'finished with engines' was rung when the ship returned to London. However, it is recalled that the readings defied precise calculation, and more often than not the mechanical counters themselves needed repairs during the round voyage.

During the long periods spent on the coast of New Zealand almost every seafarer seems to have experienced the legendary Kiwi hospitality. Going for a drink was known as a 'five to sixer' because New Zealand licensing laws in the 1960s restricted pubs to opening only from 5.00 to 6.00 pm. The rush to get a drink in after work and before going home produced a particular occasion with an atmosphere of its own. Notable were the long hoses with taps on their ends which were used to dispense beer as quickly as possible. Often whilst in port in New Zealand the engine room staff would begin overhaul work early, turning to at 6.00 am, but finishing at 12.00 noon and having the rest of the day to themselves.

Both pre-war motor ships ships survived until 1962. *Rangitata*, with her name truncated to *Rang*, made her final voyage to breakers in Yugoslavia, whilst *Rangitiki* was demolished in Spain. With their departure, the New Zealand Shipping Company felt their three post-war ships with passenger accommodation were insufficient, so bought Cunard's *Parthia*, made redundant on the North Atlantic by airline competition, and renamed her *Remuera*. But she was to make only six round voyages for the company: the great days passenger services to New Zealand were coming to an end.

Rangitata in London docks. [*Roy Fenton collection*]

Completed in 1929 by John Brown and Co. Ltd., Clydebank.
16,737 gross tons, 531 feet.
Machinery: Brown-Sulzer type ten-cylinder oil engines by John Brown and Co. Ltd., Clydebank.

Rangitata in the Dover Strait

RUAHINE
1951–1968
New Zealand Shipping Co. Ltd.

Ruahine was the last ship with passenger accommodation built for the New Zealand Shipping Company, and was to see out the company's long-standing London to Wellington service. She seems to have been something of an afterthought: the company built two larger passenger-cargo ships in 1949, *Rangitoto* and *Rangitane*, and *Ruahine* was a later and smaller version of these, with passenger accommodation reduced by a third.

Willie Watson, who was a junior engineer on *Ruahine* for her two last years in service, has very fond memories of her, but he stresses he is not looking back with rose-tinted goggles. 'The hours were long (no days off at sea), the work heavy to the point of exhaustion, and yet it was the most fulfilling time of my life', he writes.

During each four-hour watch junior engineers like Willie were in charge of running the engines and other machinery. Their seniors were on hand at all times, but the responsibility was still a heavy one for juniors in their early twenties. Willie found he had to be a quick learner, and get used to doing several things at once. There was a never-ending routine of adjustments, and near the equator the engine room temperatures would often be in excess of 100 degrees Fahrenheit. To avoid the effects of dehydration, the engineers dosed themselves with salt tablets washed down with lime juice diluted with iced water. One of Willie's tasks was to go to one of the refrigerated flats and chip ice from the evaporators in the brine room. It made a welcome relief from the oppressive heat of the engine room. Engine room dress was then down to overalls, pants, and engine room boots. Willie was perplexed that the engineers from New Zealand never wore laces in their boots.

It was not only the engineers that suffered in the heat, but also the main engines and generators. The latter were cooled by circulating fresh water, which was in turn cooled by heat exchangers in which sea water circulated. To keep the machinery at an acceptable temperature, it was necessary to shut the bypass valves to maximise the circulating cooling water. But when the ship passed through an area of cooler seawater, engine temperatures plummeted, and the by-pass valves had to be re-opened.

Then there was the 'hammer test'. This involved checking the tightness of nuts and bolts on the connecting rods, piston rods, crossheads and other parts inside the crankcase. The lubricating oil circulating pumps were shut down and the crankcase vented. Working inside the crankcase of an engine was always tricky and full of dangers for the unwary. But with an engine which had just been shut down from a long period of being 'full away' it was particularly hazardous, with internal surfaces hot to the touch and covered in a film of lubricating oil. *Ruahine's* second engineer told Willie it was 'an introduction to the finer points of marine engineering'.

As some compensation for the hard work in the engine room there were the attractions of the New Zealand coastal scenery. There was plenty of time to enjoy the landscape whilst the ship was making calls at a number of often-small ports. For instance, whilst *Ruahine* was in Queen Charlotte Sound in the South Island her skipper would take one of the ship's motor lifeboats out on the Sound, giving the engineer who accompanied the party a wonderful opportunity to experience its beauties.

Wonderful though they were for the crew, the protracted periods spent on the coast helped spell the end for cargo passenger ships. For example, on Voyage 42 *Ruahine* arrived in New Zealand on 12th December 1966, and did not depart for the United Kingdom until 3rd February, seven weeks later, during which time her passenger accommodation would be empty and the crew employed to look after them largely idle. Delays were often as a result of industrial action by dock and transportation workers. By the late 1960s, *Ruahines'* passenger accommodation was never full. Inevitably, the company announced the end of the passenger sevice in 1968. In that year *Ruahine* was sold to the Hong Kong-based shipowner C.Y. Tung and became *Oriental Rio*. She was broken up at Kaohsiung in 1973.

Ruahine on the Thames in Federal Line colours later in her career. [Ships in Focus]

Completed in 1951 by John Brown and Co. Ltd., Clydebank.
17,851 gross tons, 585 feet.
Machinery: two Doxford-type six-cylinder oil engines by John Brown and Co. Ltd., Clydebank, driving twin shafts.

Ruahine off the coast of New Zealand

SANUKI MARU
1955–1974
Nippon Yusen Kaisha, Tokyo

Japanese companies came late to shipping compared to many of their British and other European rivals, but through a combination of innovation and, it has to be said, help from their government, have outlived many of their older rivals. Nippon Yusen Kaisha (NYK) is undoubtedly Japan's premier line, and despite many difficulties has become a major force in container, bulk and reefer shipping.

NYK was part of Japan's spectacular emergence as an industrial and trading nation. The country emerged from self-inflicted isolation only in 1853 with the arrival of a US fleet under Commodore Peary. The Meiji Restoration of 1868 quickened the pace of change, and soon afterwards the Ministry of Trade was attempting to set up its own steamship service between Tokyo and Osaka. This was unsuccessful, partly due to competition from the powerful Mitsubishi organisation. The result of a later government effort, Kyodo Unyu Kaisha, merged with Mitsubishi's shipping interests in 1885, the combined company taking the title Nippon Yusen Kaisha, the Japan Mail Line. The two red bands on NYK's funnel and houseflag represent the two founding partners. A service from Japan to Europe was inaugurated in March 1896 when the *Tosa Maru* left Yokohama. Whilst Europe was distracted by the First World War, Japan was busy establishing shipyards whose products were taken by a British government desperate for ships. Japan also began to fill something of the vacuum left by withdrawal of European and US ships. Particularly fine motor passenger ships were put on services to the Pacific North West, where many Japanese had settled.

Like other Japanese fleets, that of NYK was virtually annihilated during the Second World War. This was a consequence of a disastrously flawed military and naval policy which pursued military conquests over a vast area of ocean, but could neither protect nor replace the merchant ships needed to supply these adventures. Although the unsuccessful German submarine blockades of Britain in both world wars are often discussed, the submarine war against Japan is the classic example of the vulnerability of a maritime power to such a blockade, failure of supply playing an important part in the eventual defeat of Japan.

It was not until after the 1952 peace treaty which formally ended the Second World War that Japanese shipbuilding and shipping could begin to re-establish itself. This was helped greatly by the occupying power, the USA, badly needing an ally in the Far East which was seen to be succumbing to communist domination. Secondhand ships helped to build up the Japanese fleet, and the sketch on this page shows the 1930-built steamer *Kaiyo Maru*, bought by Taiheiyo Kaiun K.K. in 1952 from British owner William Reardon Smith as *Bradburn*. Passing to other Japanese owners in 1956, Kaiyo Maru survived until 1967 when she was broken up in Japan.

NYK lost little time in re-instituting its European services, with the *Heian Maru* sailing from Yokohama in June 1952. NYK's services were built up with the help of the 15-strong 'S' class. Allocating this Japanese line berths in Birkenhead Docks, where *Sanuki Maru* is depicted in the painting, may well have given Alfred Holt, their neighbours, cause for thought. With their 17.5 knots service speed, the Japanese motor ships were worthy rivals to the Liverpool based pioneer of Far Eastern cargo liner services. Undoubtedly, competition from companies such as NYK spurred on Holts to develop faster ships in the late 1950s and 1960s.

Most of the 'S class were named after Japanese provinces, Sanuki being the ancient name for what is now Kagawa Prefecture on the island of Shikoku. *Sanuki Maru* was sold in 1974 to become *Baltic Career*, but a change of mind in 1975 saw her Greek owners rename her *Flores Career*. In June 1978 she arrived at breakers in Osaka. It is more than likely that her steel went into new hulls built in local yards, providing ships which help keep Japan's economy the second largest in the world, despite the country's late start.

Sketch of *Kaiyo Maru*.

Sanuki Maru
Completed in 1955 by Mitsubishi Zosen, Nagasaki.
9,308 gross tons, 514 feet.
Machinery: nine-cylinder oil engine by Mitsubishi Zosen, Nagasaki.

Sanuki Maru in Birkenhead Docks

ORONSAY
1951–1975
Orient Steam Navigation Co. Ltd., London

Orient Line was the premier passenger carrier between the United Kingdom and Australia, a position it had won by concentrating on large and powerful ships. From their trend-setting *Orion* of 1935, Orient evolved an admirable design, which combined, or perhaps successfully segregated, first class passengers and emigrants, 688 and 833 respectively in *Oronsay's* case.

Orion was followed in 1937 by *Orcades*, in many ways a refinement of a successful design, but sadly lost when torpedoed in the South Atlantic in October 1942. The line's first post-war newbuilding was another *Orcades*, but to an innovative external design with unconventional masts including a tripod signal mast just ahead of the funnel (see 'The British Merchant Navy: Images and Experiences' for both *Orion* and *Orcades*). *Oronsay* followed *Orcades* from the same Barrow yard, and had a number of distinctive differences, including a single mast in place of *Orcades'* tripod. *Oronsay's* birth was the more difficult, as on 28th October 1950 she caught fire whilst fitting out, a hazard with any passenger ship whose accommodation includes much inflammable material. Much water was pumped on board to staunch the blaze; indeed at one time *Oronsay* came close to capsizing. Preventing this ensured that her completion was delayed by only two months. The design was repeated one more time: *Orsova* of 1954 dispensed completely with conventional masts and was to many the most elegant of Orient's post-war ships, notwithstanding the later *Oriana*.

Ian Gibb was first officer on *Oronsay* during a Pacific cruise in the days when passenger ships took on board any mail that could be delivered along their route. At Kobe some small parcels of mail were loaded in number 4 hold and the ship departed for Hong Kong. Passing through the Straits of Formosa, smoke was seen issuing from number 4 hold. The ship's fire fighting team led by the chief officer began to investigate and passengers were sent to their lifeboat muster stations in the public rooms.

The master, Captain Roger Cutler, kept the passengers fully informed of the situation, which was not good as the fire had got such a hold that the fire fighters could barely keep it from spreading, let alone extinguish it. The sang froid of the passengers was admirable, as with every appearance of calm they sipped their afternoon tea by the swimming pool as wisps of smoke curled around them.

Fortunately, the passage to Hong Kong was short, and *Oronsay* could radio ahead to alert the local fire brigade to be waiting. But even using high expansion foam the brigade could not combat the fire, which was finally extinguished by flooding the hold from below, always a risky business as the weight of water affected the ship's stability. The source of the fire was identified as a consignment of book matches, an ill-considered item to send by mail.

From this experience Ian Gibb learned that the best thing to do in an emergency was to keep the passengers and crew fully informed. The reward for the captain would be a calm and efficient solution to the problem. The lesson stood Ian in good stead when, years later, he was master of *Canberra* when she caught fire off Madras.

In 1954 *Oronsay* made the first trans-Pacific voyages for Orient Line, initiating the connection with British Colombia and California which was to become a major part of the company's future itinerary. Joe Chapman joined *Oronsay* in the early summer of 1961 as second officer at the start of her cruising season from Southampton. The ship established another first during that season with a two-day visit to Odessa. Though the cold war was much in evidence the people were extremely friendly, many having a good command of English and being willing to talk. In the evening four officers were invited to a performance of 'The Sleeping Beauty' in the magnificent Opera House. They were seated in the Royal Box and at every interval the double doors at the back were opened and they were guided up marble stairs to a salon where champagne and caviar were served. It remains in Joe's memory as the most imperialist experience of his career.

By the time Joe was next appointed to *Oronsay*, this time as chief officer in 1968, many things had changed. Orient Line and P&O had merged, white paint covered the original corn-coloured hull, a number of the European stewards had been replaced by Goanese, whilst professional singers, dancers, musicians, conjurors, comedians and lecturers entertained the passengers.

Despite her unfortunate start in life, *Oronsay* was the longest serving of the three Orient liners built at Barrow in the immediate post-war years, surviving until April 1976 when demolition began at Kaohsiung.

Oronsay in home waters. [J. & M. Clarkson]

Built 1951 by Vickers-Armstrongs Ltd., Barrow-in-Furness.
27,632 gross tons, 682 feet.
Machinery: six Pametrada-type geared turbines by Vickers-Armstrongs Ltd., Barrow-in-Furness, driving twin shafts.

Oronsay at sea

IBERIA

1954–1972

P&O Steam Navigation Company, London

Iberia was the fourth passenger vessel in P&O's extensive post-war reconstruction programme. Even the largest shipping company in the world at the time did not have the resources to replace all its ships, but P&O had no choice but to rebuild their fleet. As the company reported to a public enquiry in 1968, 'They had to replace their ships to regain their trades, or see them taken by others for good, and so they replaced, but at high pressure and at costs enormously greater than the value of the insurance which they had received for tonnage lost during the War...'.

P&O's strategy was to build fewer but faster vessels. For instance, the voyage time on the London to Australia service for which *Iberia* was destined was reduced by eight days with ships which could steam at 22 knots. *Iberia* and her near-sister *Arcadia* were ordered in 1951 earlier than intended, because P&O feared that the demand for shipping stimulated by the Korean War might mean building berths would soon become unavailable. She was to be the last of what might be described as P&O's conventional liners, as she was followed albeit seven years later by the innovative, engines-aft *Canberra* (*Arcadia* and *Canberra* are both featured in 'The British Merchant Navy: Images and Experiences').

Iberia's one moment of infamy came in March 1956 when she was in collision with the tanker *Stanvac Pretoria* whilst heading for the Ceylonese port of Colombo at about 00.30 hours. Ian Gibb was Senior Cadet on *Iberia* and, like most cadets, slept very well, so he never heard the collision nor the ringing of bells and activity which followed. On arriving on the bridge at 08.00 expecting to see land, he was surprised to see that Ceylon was not even on the horizon. The first officer led him to the port bridge wing and directed his attention to where damaged boats and davits were hanging over the ship's side. *Iberia* was so badly damaged that repairs were instituted by the Cockatoo Dockyard soon after she arrived at Sydney. Ian was given the job of coordinating plans and

keeping a logbook of repairs. He found this experience invaluable, not long before getting his first 'ticket', although he was never again involved in a collision at sea during a career of 40 years,

Iberia was not a completely successful ship. Despite being a near sister to *Arcadia*, she was much less stable, and is reputed to have come near to capsizing on at least one occasion. In addition, she did not have sufficient distillation capacity to provide fresh water whilst making a crossing of the Pacific, and on such voyages water had to be rationed, which was very unpopular with passengers. These problems meant that in 1970 *Arcadia* rather than *Iberia* was chosen from the pair for conversion to a one-class ship to better suit her for the cruising role, which was becoming increasingly important to P&O.

The company was increasingly aware that standards of accommodation plus good marketing were essential if they were to fill their ships. The chairman, Sir Donald Anderson, reported to the 1967 AGM that 'The days are long past when the Company's staff sat patiently behind the stone portals of lofty booking halls, waiting for passengers to book passages to distant parts of the world. P&O has to face up to the fact that the fleet of 11 passenger vessels has more accommodation to sell than any hotel group in the country...'.

As it became increasingly difficult to fill this vast number of cabins, P&O began to thin out its fleet. In view of her problems, and her out-dated two-class accommodation, *Iberia* was one of the first victims. In September 1972 she was sold to breakers in Taiwan at the early age of 18.

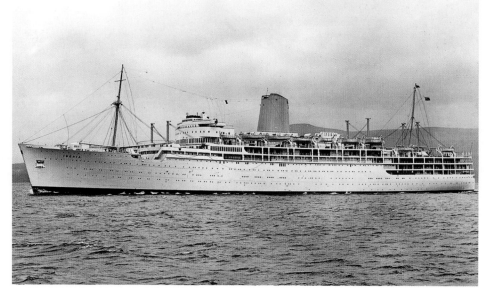

Iberia running trials on the Clyde. *[Roy Fenton collection]*

Completed in 1954 by Harland and Wolff Ltd., Belfast.
29,614 gross tons, 719 feet.
Machinery: six steam turbines by Harland and Wolff Ltd., Belfast, double-reduction geared to twin shafts.

Iberia outward bound off the Needles

PORT AUCKLAND
1949–1976
Port Line Ltd, London

Port Auckland was one of the finest looking British cargo liners of post-war years, no small achievement given that the design of such ships reached its zenith in this period. Port Auckland, with her slightly earlier sister, Port Brisbane, created a whole new image for the Australian and New Zealand services of Port Line. With their streamlined bridge front and funnel, and long forecastles with generous applications of white paint, they could be mistaken for miniature passenger ships, although they had cabins for just 12. Much of the credit for the design must go to Swan, Hunter and Wigham Richardson Ltd. who did much of the development work for Port Brisbane.

The design was developed and continued right through and beyond the 1950s, the initial pair being followed by a dozen more. However, in most of these ships the bridge deck was extended forward, which interrupted the curving line of the bridge, and the Port Auckland and her sister remained the most elegant Port Line ships.

The company's homeward trade was essentially in foodstuffs including frozen mutton and lamb, butter and cheese, plus seasonal consignments of wool. Port Auckland therefore had a large proportion of her cargo space refrigerated, five of her six holds. At 17 knots she also had a good turn of speed to bring this cargo back to Europe. Something of an innovation for a British cargo liner was a deck crane, serving numbers 4 and 5 hatches, although this feature was soon to become almost standard.

John Burtt remembers Port Line as an exceedingly good company to work for, with well-found, comfortable ships, good pay and food well above the average, especially on the ships that carried passengers. He has a vivid memory of his time on the Port Wyndham of 1935, which in 1962 had loaded in New York two 12-metre yachts which were on their way back to Sydney after an unsuccessful Australian challenge for the America's Cup. Carried as deck cargo, the yachts were on cradles and had all their masts and rigging

stripped. This was the time of the Cuban missile crisis, with the USA extremely concerned about Russian ships being on their way to Cuba with consignments of missiles. The Port Wyndham's deck cargo might, just, have been taken for missiles, and the ship was constantly buzzed by nervous US aircraft and destroyers. This was before the days of VHF radio, and Port Wyndham had to resort to sending reassuring messages by Aldis lamp whenever they received the challenge 'What ship? Where bound? What is your cargo?'

The specialist nature of Port Line's trade meant that there were few buyers for their ships when containerisation began in the 1970s. Two of her running mates underwent dramatic conversions to cruise ships, but Port Auckland's new role was more humble. In 1976 she was sold to a Kuwait owner and taken to Keppel Shipyard in Singapore for conversion to carry sheep on the hoof. In the Middle East and elsewhere meat has to be slaughtered according to certain religious rituals, so the unfortunate animals have to be transported alive. The former Port Auckland therefore continued to serve the Australian farmers as Mashaallah (her name is translated as 'God is wonderful', but whether the sheep shared this sentiment is debatable). There was continuity of management, too, with the ship run by Cunard Brocklebank, the style under which Port Line's owners now operated their much diminished fleet. Whether her conversion was worthwhile must be doubted, however, as after only three years the 30-year-old Mashaallah was broken up Kaohsiung. Port Line outlived her by only a few years, and by 1983 the company title and its distinctive ships had gone.

Port Auckland as Mashaallah, the conversion to a sheep carrier having changed her outward appearance very little. [M.R. Dippy]

Completed in 1949 by R. and W. Hawthorn, Leslie and Co. Ltd., Newcastle-upon-Tyne.
11,945 gross tons, 560 feet overall.
Machinery: Doxford-type six-cylinder oil engine by R. and W. Hawthorn, Leslie and Co. Ltd., Newcastle-upon-Tyne.

Port Auckland at Port Chalmers

KONG HAAKON VII

1969–1984

R/A Julian (Hilmar Reksten, manager), Bergen

One can imagine the headlines: 'Three of the world's biggest tankers blow up within two weeks'. What is more, these disasters happened in the same area of sea, off the west coast of Africa. Nowadays, terrorism would be strongly suspected, but the culprit turned out to be rather different. It was a case of ship construction being pushed too far and too fast.

It is difficult to chart exactly when tankers began to increase in size. As far back as 1912 the Eagle Oil Company was ordering tankers of 16,000 deadweight tons, considered to be the largest in the world, but in the 1950s began a seemingly-unstoppable inflation in tanker sizes. In November 1953, the *Tina Onassis* of 45,000 deadweight tons was the world's largest, but just six years later the first 100,000 tonner, *Universe Apollo*, was on order. The ultimate tanker – or ultra-large crude carrier as they began to be called – was the *Seawise Giant*, the result of rebuilding a 410,000 into a 560,000 tonner. As *Jahre Viking* this vessel is featured on page 102 of this book.

The *Kong Haakon VII* was ordered at the height of the feverish rush to build ever larger crude carriers. When delivered in August 1969 she was both the largest ship built in Norway and the biggest in the Norwegian fleet, a fleet in which tankers had been an important component since the 1930s.

Just five months later, on 12th December 1969, Shell's 100,000 ton *Marpessa* was sailing off the coast of Africa, having recently discharged her first cargo of oil in Europe. She never loaded another cargo of Arabian crude, as a massive explosion occurred in one of her centre tanks, killing two of her crew and injuring others. The explosion severed the deck lines that carried water for fire fighting and it became impossible to extinguish the fire resulting from the explosion. *Marpessa's* bulkheads began to collapse, and she sank three days after the initial explosion. More was to follow. Within two weeks, her sister *Mactra* and the *Kong Haakon VII* suffered similar explosions, although both remained afloat.

The geographical proximity of these explosions was no coincidence. The ships were all cleaning their cargo tanks at this stage of the voyage, and tank cleaning equipment came under immediate suspicion. One theory was that metal grinding on metal had caused a spark that ignited the mixture of air and gas left in the tanks when the crude had been discharged. However, further research suggested another explanation. So large were the cargo tanks that they generated their own weather, including thunderstorms. Water washing techniques generated large static charges in the tanks, resulting in the equivalent of a lightning strike which ignited the gas and air mixture.

Oil shippers quickly took steps to control the atmosphere in tanks using gas-freeing techniques or blanketing with inert carbon dioxide produced by the ship's engines. There have been no more major explosions in large crude carriers, but the problem has not gone away. A number of smaller tankers and tank barges have suffered accidents which have been put down to static discharge giving rise to an explosion.

The further history of vessels like *Kong Haakon VII* was more often than not blighted. The Arab-Israel War of 1973 precipitated an oil crisis, which left too many large tankers chasing too little oil. Tanker freight rates collapsed, deep water berths in Norway and elsewhere filled with laid up tankers, and owners of vessels such as *Kong Haakon VII* went bankrupt. Shipbuilders, too, were affected as orders were cancelled and the huge docks designed to build even bigger tankers went idle. The public's image of large tankers was not helped by disasters such as when the *Amoco Cadiz* was wrecked off the French coast causing massive pollution, or the drunken master of the *Exxon Valdez* contaminated King William's Sound in Alaska. *Kong Haakon VII* was broken up in 1984, and although large crude carriers continue to have an important place in the world's shipping, it is unlikely that there will be another feverish rush to build ever bigger tankers.

Completed in 1969 by Akers A/S Stord Werft, Lervik.
109,422 gross tons, 1,075 feet.
Machinery: two GEC-type steam turbines by Kvaerner Brug A/S, Oslo, geared to a single shaft.

Kong Haakon VII.

Kong Haakon VII at Lisbon, and showing explosion damage

ANDES

1939–1971

Royal Mail Lines Ltd., London

A*ndes* was Royal Mail's flagship for many years, and is remembered with tremendous affection by many who sailed on her. However, like other ships of her era, her birth was clouded by economic and political uncertainty.

In 1932 Lord Essendon, Chairman of the newly-created Royal Mail Lines Ltd., made an exhaustive survey of the line's major passenger service to the River Plate ports. He concluded that Royal Mail's goodwill would soon cease to exist unless it introduced up-to-date tonnage, because 22-knot French and German vessels were offering passages which were five days faster. If money could be obtained – and the Chairman acknowledged it was a big if given the prevailing economic conditions – the ideal would be to build a 23-knot ship. But he doubted whether this was justified, as he believed their competitors were also losing large sums of money.

One solution was to threaten the competitors with building a fast new ship, and invite them to agree to limit speed on the River Plate service to 19 knots. For Royal Mail's existing ships to achieve this speed, however, they would need re-engining, which was somewhat embarrassing as *Asturias* and *Alcantara* had failed to achieve their contract speed when new, a situation never rectified because of the rather cosy relationship between Royal Mail and builders Harland and Wolff. In the event, agreement was reached with the rivals, the two ships were revitalised by having turbines installed, and plans for the new ship – *Andes* – were shelved for a few years.

Construction of the new ship was periodically re-examined and finally approved in September 1936. Harland and Wolff submitted the lowest bid, but at £1,365,000 it was still 'very much in excess of anticipations'. The *Andes* was due to make her maiden voyage from Southampton to South America on 26th September 1939, the 100th anniversary of the granting of a royal charter to the original Royal Mail Steam Packet Company. But the outbreak of the Second World War meant that she went instead to Liverpool, where her new fittings were mostly removed so that she could become a troopship. Two of her notable achievements on war service were returning the Norwegian government in exile to Oslo in 1945 and

establishing a record passage from Southampton to Bombay of 13½ days in July 1946. Her maiden peacetime voyage was not made until January 1948.

With little post-war competition from continental lines, *Andes* soon established herself on the South American run, and in the affections of her crew. One expression of the spirit onboard was 'The Dolphin', the ship's magazine produced by members of the crew. Initially duplicated, but later printed ashore during the five days the ship was in Buenos Aires each voyage, 'The Dolphin' was produced for well over one hundred voyages.

Although *Andes* was considered a 'happy ship', things ashore were going much less well, and it was felt that Royal Mail management were not doing a good job. There were problems aplenty in their trades, but some decisions were highly questionable, including that to build three new passenger-cargo ships for the River Plate trade at a time when passengers were deserting the sea for the air, and economic and political problems in South America meant cargo shipments were uncertain.

Replaced by new ships, in 1959 *Andes* went to the De Schelde yard at Vlissingen, Holland to be turned into a one-class cruise ship. From 324 first and 204 second class passengers, her accommodation was reduced somewhat to 480 in one class. Her bridge deck was extended fore and aft, and a major change was the adoption of a white hull.

Jim Lee recalls the last three cruises *Andes* which undertook as being bedevilled by boiler trouble. It was a particular problem to him as Shore Excursion Manager, as these problems meant her itinerary was constantly changing. On the final cruise, to the West Indies, some of the stops had to be missed and even then she returned to Southampton a day late. On arrival, her launches were removed and she was sold to breakers in Ghent for £300,000, leaving in February 1971. She had to be partly flooded in order to pass beneath one of the bridges on the Ghent Canal: an undignified end to the 40-year story of a splendid ship.

Andes as a white-hulled cruise ship. [J. & M. Clarkson]

Completed in 1939 by Harland and Wolff Ltd., Belfast.
26,689 gross tons, 669 feet.
Machinery: two sets each of three steam turbines by Harland and Wolff Ltd., Belfast, single-reduction geared to twin shafts.

Andes off the Needles

EBRO

1952–1969

Royal Mail Lines Ltd., London

Ebro and her three near-sisters worked Royal Mail's service from UK to Jamaica and the romantically titled Spanish Main, a route dating from the origins of this celebrated company.

Lanarkshire-born founder James MacQueen (1778-1870) managed estates in the West Indies, and as an avid traveller became convinced that steam navigation had an enormous potential for inter-island communication in the Caribbean. He took his ideas further, envisaging a global network of steamer services. A very determined man, in 1838 MacQueen approached the treasury with a proposal for a Royal Mail Line of steamers to the West Indies to speed the delivery of mails, which was still in the hands of slow and unreliable Admiralty brigs. Perhaps surprisingly, his ideas were quickly accepted, and in July 1839 the Royal Mail Steam Packet Company was incorporated by royal charter, gaining the government mail contract early in 1840. In January 1842 the *Thames* steamed out of Falmouth with the first mails, her route extended from the West Indies (where schooners distributed the mails) to New York and Halifax, Nova Scotia. As well as North America, Royal Mail also extended its routes to South America.

By the beginning of the twentieth century, the company was at a low ebb, despite its mail contracts and its prestigious royal charter which gave it similar safeguards to a limited liability concern. Part of the problem was that the company had inherited many ways of doing things from the Royal Navy; it even had an admiral for a chairman. But in January 1903 a tramp ship owner named Owen Philipps joined the board, and such was his dynamism that within three months he was to become chairman. Philipps, later Lord Kylsant, reinvigorated the Royal Mail company, and set out on a policy of acquisition that within two decades made the Royal Mail Group one of Britain's and the world's major shipping combines. The story was to end in tears in the late 1920s, but in his time Kylsant was a major figure in shipping, and his dubious accountancy was balanced by his influence in getting the motor vessel established in the British merchant fleet.

In 1932 Royal Mail Lines Ltd. emerged out of the wreckage of the Royal Mail Group and settled down to being a modest-sized company operating to South American and Caribbean ports. The company's association with Harland

and Wolff was maintained and in the 1950s they built the *Ebro* and her three later near-sisters, *Essequibo*, *Escalante* and *Eden*.

Kingston, Jamaica was one of the most important ports the 'E' ships served and indeed, Royal Mail had their own wharf there. The ships often discharged spirits at Kingston with at least one apprentice watching each hold in an attempt to reduce pilferage, and usually loaded sugar for the homeward voyage to London or Liverpool. It was a favourite port for a run ashore, and some of the characters and locations have passed into Royal Mail folklore. Royal Mail personnel were particularly welcome to enjoy Appleton's rum in Doris' Drinking Saloon, describing itself slightly paradoxically as 'The cosiest hot spot in town'.

Also remembered with affection is Miss Ella, an elderly fruit lady of an amiable disposition and with a fascinating vocabulary: 'I's gwine out to de man-o-war' meant she was heading for a naval ship in the bay. Ella ran a group of washer women, including two who were dubbed Snow White and Pearl, who enquired of the crew 'Can a do ya landry, Mr Deep?' David Cobbold remembers the time when Snow White took a bundle of whites for the master of the *Ebro*, but when they were returned the skipper's tiger discovered three sets were missing. David had to find Snow White and bring her before the captain. 'Even dee Lord can forgive, mon' she exclaimed before offering an explanation involving scorching the whites whilst they were being ironed.

Between 1968 and 1970, all four of the 'E' group were sold for further trading. *Ebro* became the *Fortune Victory* for Hong Kong owners in 1969, later joining the Burma Five Star Line as *Kalemyo*. She was broken up in mainland China late in 1978. Royal Mail Lines Ltd. passed into the control of the Furness group in 1965 and soon all that were left were a few ships with traditional river names. However, a flourishing Royal Mail Association keeps former employees in touch, and memories alive of one of the great names in British shipping.

Completed in 1952 by Harland and Wolff Ltd., Govan.
7,784 gross tons, 445 feet.
Machinery: six-cylinder oil engine by Harland and Wolff Ltd., Govan.

Ebro in the English Channel. [J. & M. Clarkson collection]

Ebro at Port of Spain

SOUTHERN CROSS

1955–1973

Shaw, Savill and Albion Co. Ltd., London

Southern Cross can be genuinely described as a revolutionary ship. Her concept as a pure passenger ship freed her designers to employ her hull space to best advantage for her passengers, and this resulted in an entirely new profile, which has since become very familiar.

The novelty of the *Southern Cross* was that she was a pure passenger ship. The reasoning was that discharging cargo took far longer than disembarking passengers, especially when the former meant visiting several ports. Many of the large numbers of crew employed solely to look after passengers were idle when the cabins were empty. There were also difficulties ensuring the orderly delivery of cargo to the ship, and these caused a conflict of interest. Did the ship keep faith with its passengers, and sail on schedule even if part of its cargo capacity was unfilled? Or did it delay sailings to maximise its cargo earnings, and risk the ire of passengers who sailed late? The solution decided upon by Chairman Basil Sanderson and his Shaw, Savill colleagues was to consign freight to pure cargo ships, and build a ship that could carry 1,164 passengers and make four round voyages a year from the UK to Australia and New Zealand. In contrast, a cargo-passenger ship would be lucky to make three voyages annually.

With no cargo space needed, the designers had a relatively free hand. Turbines and boilers, together with the funnel, were placed aft, so the best and roomiest part of the ship was available for passenger accommodation. The absence of cargo holds and engine uptakes amidships removed restrictions on the size and design of public rooms. Deck space for passenger use was maximised: the area of the sports deck was particularly generous, and there were two swimming pools. Placing the engines aft posed the question of how to trim the vessel evenly, allowing for the consumption of bunker oil. As the fuel was used up, it was replaced by distilled water supplied by a plant producing 300 tons per day, thus maintaining the vessel's trim.

Southern Cross was named by the Queen on 17th August 1954, and this was another unique occasion: the first time a British merchant ship had been launched by a reigning monarch. *Southern Cross* left Southampton on her maiden voyage on 29th March 1955 under

the command of Sir David Aitchison, who had been knighted for his command of *Gothic* which carried the Queen on her tour of Australia and New Zealand.

The success of the ship can be judged by the decision taken to build a near sister, the appropriately named *Northern Star* completed in 1962. Fifty feet longer and with accommodation for 1,400 passengers, *Northern Star* benefited from experience with *Southern Cross* and, for instance, no cabins were sited beneath the Tavern, a popular place for late night partying. Captain Edward Buckle had experience of both ships, but felt that *Southern Cross* was the better sea ship, which could ride a short swell in the Australian Bight with ease. With being a little smaller, she seemed more solid in her construction. She was probably the happier of the two, and the understanding between officers and ratings gave a wonderful working environment seldom found in ships with such large crews and a credit to the heads of departments. Edward feels he was privileged to have sailed in the *Southern Cross*, in a position where he could admire the vision of her designers, the pride in their workmanship of those who built her, and the efficiency of the routine set up during her early voyages. He writes that, just as the constellation after which she was named remains fixed in the sky, so the memories of the *Southern Cross* will remain embedded in the hearts and minds of all who sailed in her.

In 1973 *Southern Cross* was retired from Shaw, Savill service, the airliner having taken most of her trade (the younger *Northern Star* was retired two years later, but went straight to the breakers). *Southern Cross* found a Greek buyer and, converted to a cruise ship, sailed on and on, initially as *Calypso*, from 1980 as *Azure Seas*, and from 1992 as *Oceanbreeze*, a name she still carries. Even more than her remark-able survival, she has had a lasting influence on passenger ship design, as witness the *Canberra* and the majority of today's cruise ships.

Southern Cross on trials. [Roy Fenton collection]

Completed in 1955 by Harland and Wolff Ltd., Belfast.
20,204 gross tons, 604 feet.
Machinery: four Pametrada-type steam turbines by Harland and Wolff Ltd., Belfast, double-reduction geared to two shafts.

Southern Cross in the Pacific

KUNGSHOLM

1966–1975

A/B Svenska Amerika Linien, Gothenburg

Kungsholm was one of the last and most graceful transatlantic liners. Sadly, she was too late, but found a successful new role as a cruise ship. Owners Swedish-Amerika Line were relative late-comers to the North Atlantic, their forerunners the Rederi Sverige Nordamerika purchasing their first ship for the Gothenburg-New York route in 1915. Swedish-Amerika, as the company became in 1922, used the name Kungsholm for the first time in that year for a former Dutch vessel. By the 1960s it was apparent that fewer and fewer passengers were crossing the Atlantic by sea, and the future for big passenger ships lay increasingly with cruising. In common with other companies who felt their prestige rested on continuing North Atlantic services, Swedish-Amerika designed a ship which could be used for liner voyages for part of the year, but would be suitable for cruising for around 80 percent of her time. Cunard were reaching the same decision about this time, but it was Swedish-Amerika who got in first with their order, oddly going to the Clydebank yard, John Brown, who were later to build the Queen Elizabeth 2.

The new Kungsholm was a handsome ship, with her clipper bow, cruiser stern, two well raked masts, and – a controversial feature – two funnels, the forward of which was a dummy. She could accommodate 750 passengers in two classes, but this was reduced to 450 in one class when cruising. She had no capacity for cargo. Kungsholm was described by the chairman of the owners as '...one of the finest we have ever received from any shipyard', but it was a shame that John Brown tarnished their reputation by delivering the ship four months late. She was moved from the Clyde to Gothenburg for the installation of Swedish furniture and other fittings, before leaving for her maiden voyage on 22nd April 1966.

That she was really built too late is shown by the passenger figures for her maiden voyage: just 304, meaning that even on this auspicious occasion she was less than half full. Nevertheless, she continued with her owners for

nine years, concentrating more and more on cruising during this period.

Swedish-Amerika withdrew from passenger shipping in August 1975, and sold Kungsholm to a New York-based company who put her under the Panama flag, but did not alter her name. She cruised out of New York for three years.

In 1978 P&O were looking for a replacement for their 1954-built Arcadia, which had been adapted as a cruise ship in 1973. P&O bought Kungsholm and sent her for a major refit at Bremen, which cost almost twice as much as she had to build 12 years earlier. This high price was surprising, as the public rooms were altered in name only, and the major change involved extending some cabins and fitting others. The refit meant loss of her forward dummy funnel, with the remaining one being raised in height, which some observers regretted as altering her classic lines, but it undoubtedly modernised her appearance. She emerged as Sea Princess, owned by P&O's subsidiary, Princess Cruises.

In a symbolic move, Sea Princess did physically replace Arcadia. The two ships met at Keppel Harbour, Singapore in February 1979, and passengers were transferred from Arcadia to Sea Princess, the former then going to breakers, whilst the Sea Princess

Victoria, the former Kungsholm, in the Solent.

concluded the cruise. This positioned the new ship at Sydney, from where she was to work for the next three years. Since then she has worked out of Southampton and the west coast of the USA, with periodic refits.

In 1995 she was renamed Victoria, P&O reviving an old and more distinguished name than Sea Princess as they transferred her to P&O Cruises. In 2002 she was sold, but has continued to cruise as Mona Lisa under the Bahamas flag. As in the case of Southern Cross, she is a marvellous example of a soundly built ship being capable of prolonged and demanding service.

Completed in 1966 by John Brown and Co. (Clydebank) Ltd., Clydebank.
26,678 gross tons, 660 feet.
Machinery: two nine-cylinder oil engines by A/B Gotaverken, Gothenburg.

Kungsholm fitting out at Clydebank

CARNARVON CASTLE

1926–1962

Union-Castle Mail Steamship Co. Ltd., London

Carnarvon Castle in her war paint is a reminder of just how important was the Merchant Navy to Britain's Second World War effort. Victory against fascism would have been much more difficult, if not impossible, without the ships, and even more the men and women who served in them. Let it not be forgotten that losses in the Merchant Navy were higher as a percentage of persons enrolled than in the Army, Royal Navy or Royal Air Force.

Carnarvon Castle was Union-Castle's first diesel-driven mail ship, a decision which had everything to do with the enthusiasm of then owner, Lord Kylsant, for motor ships, and his close association with Lord Pirrie of Harland and Wolff. In her first manifestation Carnarvon Castle was a typical, rather understated, Pirrie-Kylsant ship, with two squat funnels and straight stem, all of which belied her size as Union-Castle's biggest mail ship.

A new mail contract signed in 1936 required the voyage time between Southampton and Cape Town to be reduced to under 14 days. This required new ships, and upgrading of old ones. In 1937 Carnarvon Castle was returned to her builders and re-engined, increasing her speed to over 20 knots and allowing her to win the record for the southbound voyage to South Africa from Stirling Castle, her time being a very creditable 12 days, 13 hours. Just as impressive was the change in her appearance. She now had an elegant, almost clipper-like, bow and a single larger and well-proportioned funnel.

She was to serve in this new guise for less than two years, as on the outbreak of war in 1939 she was immediately requisitioned by the Admiralty. The dockyard at Simon's Town converted her into an armed merchant cruiser, equipping her with eight 6-inch guns and two 3-inch guns. The accompanying painting recalls the occasion when a mine bounced alongside Carnarvon Castle's hull, fortunately failing to explode.

The guns fitted to British armed merchant cruisers generally dated from the previous war, or even earlier. In fact, their German opponents had similarly antique weapons, usually all that was left in Germany after the

surrendered High Seas Fleet had scuttled itself at Scapa Flow. There was one important difference, however: the German mountings were either new or updated, and usually could far outrange those of British armed merchant cruisers. The German auxiliary Thor demonstrated this dramatically off Trinidad in July 1940 when she outranged and outfought the British armed merchant cruiser Alcantara. In December 1940, Thor was intercepted by Carnarvon Castle. The latter's gunnery control system was put out of action early in the fight by a combination of luck and good shooting by her opponent. Carnarvon Castle's guns were left to fire independently, a very haphazard situation, and contributed to her getting the worst of this single-ship action, being hit 27 times before her smaller opponent broke off the action.

Experiences like this made the Admiralty rethink the use of extremely valuable passenger ships as makeshift cruisers, and at one time they proposed converting her to an aircraft carrier – and this was in fact done with the Pretoria Castle. Instead, and much more sensibly, Carnarvon Castle was handed over to the Ministry of War Transport in November 1943 and converted to a troopship. She remained in what must have been a fairly basic state internally well after her return to Union-Castle in 1947, when she began an emigrant service to South Africa, offering 1,293 berths in comparison with 850 with which she had been designed. A major refit in 1949 allowed her to return to the mail service, with a much more civilised complement of 216 first and 401 tourist class passengers.

In 1962 the arrival of the new mail ship Transvaal Castle made her surplus to requirements, and Carnarvon Castle sailed out to Japan and the shipbreakers. The years from 1950 were probably the best for a rather ugly duckling that judicious rebuilding had transformed into a swan.

Built in 1926 by Harland and Wolff Ltd., Belfast. 20,063 gross tons, 631 feet.
Machinery: two Burmeister & Wain-type eight-cylinder oil engines by Harland and Wolff Ltd., Belfast, driving twin shafts. Replaced in 1937 with 10-cylinder engines of increased power.

Carnarvon Castle as built.

Carnarvon Castle as an armed merchant cruiser during the Second World War

AMERICAN HARVESTER
1948–1968
United States Lines Company, New York

The story of United States Lines began with one failure, and ended with another. Following the First World War, the ex-German passenger ships which the United States government had impounded on declaring war on Germany in 1917 were chartered to the United States Mail Steamship Company. The company's services from New York to Europe collapsed dismally after just one year and the US government took the vessels back, forming United States Lines to operate them on the same routes. Although many newer ships were acquired, United States Lines was no more successful than its predecessor at operating North Atlantic services at a profit, and only US government ownership kept it afloat. In 1929 the Government sold the company and in 1931 its fleet became part of the International Mercantile Marine. This US-based multinational will be remembered as one-time owner of White Star and other lines.

Losses during the Second World War were grave and, with its passenger ships taken up as troop transports, the fleet of United States Lines reached its lowest numerical strength. But the massive US merchant ship construction programme of the Second World War saw it completely rejuvenated.

The United States Lines' post-war cargo fleet comprised around 50 war-built standard ships, mostly of the C2 type. Many of these were completed for United States Lines with *American* names, others being acquired in early post-war years, including *Rattler* which became *American Harvester*.

Ports used by the *Americans* on the eastern seaboard included Hampton Roads, Baltimore, Philadelphia, New York and Boston, whilst most major European ports in the range Bilbao to Hamburg were served. Reflecting the economic difficulties US ships had in the years immediately after the First World War, United States Lines received a government subsidy for its services. Throughout the 1950s and early 1960s, the company maintained its North Atlantic services exclusively with the C2s, mostly built in 1945. It was criticised for keeping obsolete

tonnage, but its riposte was that it was awaiting containerisation.

As the C2s were replaced with more modern tonnage, they were transferred to a new subsidiary, American Leader Inc. Ostensibly these ships were now tramping, but all were chartered by the US military, which was fully engaged in the Vietnam War. *American Harvester* became *Mystic Mariner* in 1968, and was scrapped at Kaohsiung in 1971.

United States Lines began containerising in 1969, and such were the savings that just six container ships could replace 23 conventional cargo liners. With the 1980s seeing container ships growing in size, and competition increasing, United States Lines determined on re-establishing its leadership. It ordered a dozen vessels from Daewoo in South Korea designed to maintain a bi-weekly round-the-world service. They were to be the world's largest container vessels, and the order was said to be the most expensive ever placed for merchant ships. The new ships reversed the trend of ever-greater speeds and were designed to be driven at a modest, though economical, 18 knots. This was to be one of the costliest misjudgements in shipping history. The calculation that fuel price rises would make uneconomic the faster container ships ordered by competitors proved wide of the mark. The comparatively slow round-the-world service lost out, especially to Evergreen Lines, and United States Lines faced financial ruin. In 1986 it recognised that it was bankrupt and filed for protection from its creditors. The big new container ships were laid up or sold and the once-great fleet of United States Lines simply withered away. Its demise is a reminder that the modern shipping world is not a place for the financially meek, and is one where misjudgements can be massively expensive.

Completed in 1945 by North Carolina Ship Building Company, Wilmington.
8,287 gross tons, 441 feet.
Machinery: two steam turbines by General Electric Company, Lynn, Massachusetts, double-reduction geared to one shaft.

American Harvester in the Thames. [Ships in Focus]

American Harvester approaches New York

UNITED STATES
1952–1969
United States Lines Company, New York

*U*nited States was a ship which attracted superlatives: the fastest conventional passenger ship ever built, the last genuine holder of the blue ribband, and perhaps one of the most heavily subsidised ships ever. She was one of the last ships conceived for North Atlantic liner voyages rather than as a part-time cruise ship, but had many features of a troop ship.

Her genesis lay in a directive from President Roosevelt in October 1944 which proposed no fewer than 11 'superliners' to be built after the war for service on all important trade routes. However, in the post-war world it was apparent that passenger ships would experience competition from airliners, and only six ships from this programme were to be built, including the *United States*.

Her naval architect William Gibbs saw the ship as a machine, whilst she was seen as a military asset by the US government who were footing the bill. Military considerations meant she had to be capable of transiting the Panama Canal, which kept her length below that of Cunard's Queens. Potentially she could carry 14,000 troops, and had a 400-bed hospital. Watertight doors were fitted as far up as A deck and, in an effort to reduce the risk of fire, wood was virtually eliminated, only her butchers' blocks and pianos escaping this rule. She had two completely separate engine rooms, which could operate independently if one were disabled by enemy action.

But it was her performance that was truly superlative, although it was only later in her life that this ceased being a state secret. It was achieved by cramming the biggest power plant into the lightest possible hull (aluminium was extensively used) made possible by what writer Peter Kohler described as 'an inexhaustible budget.' Her power meant the *United States* would make a sensational debut. On her maiden voyage from New York to Southampton in July 1952 she averaged 35.59 knots, convincingly taking the blue ribband from the *Queen Mary* with a voyage time of just under three and a half days from the Ambrose Light to the Bishop Rock. Her return voyage set a westbound record. A British journalist wrote that 'After the loud and fantastic claims

made in advance for the liner, it comes as something as a disappointment to find them all true'. In fact, the *United States* had achieved these record crossings with power in hand. In 1968 it was revealed that her turbines were rated at 240,000 shaft horse power, and could drive her at 42 knots.

United States had only a few good years in service. Passenger loadings were excellent through the 1950s, so much so that in 1957 the US government made plans to build a sister ship. But in 1958 the first transatlantic service by jet aircraft was inaugurated by BOAC, and suddenly the era of the passenger ship was over. By 1960 competition was hurting the *United States*, as was frequent industrial action by those crewing and handling her. But what finally killed the ship's career was her enormous operating cost, Peter Kohler describing her as 'consuming more government subsidy than oil'. In 1969 during the Vietnam War (when she was conspicuously not used as a troop transport), President Johnson pulled the plug on the subsidy, and *United States* was laid up not far from her building berth.

This was by no means the end of her story, as 36 years on the *United States* is still with us, currently in Philadelphia. Much that has happened during the last two thirds of her career has involved accountants, lawyers, bureaucrats and politicians, and the only real progress to putting her back into service was made by the Turkish and Ukrainean workers who stripped out her asbestos in the 1990s. Far too expensive to return to service without a massive government subsidy, yet too much of an icon to be broken up, the *United States* lingers on in her persistent vegetative state, a victim of the superlatives surrounding her.

United States passes the second *Mauretania*.

Completed in 1952 by the Newport News Shipbuilding and Drydock Company, Newport News.
38,216 gross tons, 990 feet.
Machinery: four steam turbines by Westinghouse Electrical and Manufacturing Company, Easington, Pennsylvania, double-reduction geared to quadruple shafts.

United States and the *Queen Mary*, the ship from which she took the blue ribband on her 1952 maiden voyage

ALDABI

1946–1967

Van Nievelt Goudriaan & Co's Stoomvaartmaatschappij, Rotterdam

Aldabi was born at an inauspicious time. Launched in Amsterdam on 23rd November 1940, she was still incomplete when the Netherlands was invaded, and she was confiscated by the Germans at the outfitting quay on 7th August 1941. Work did not proceed quickly, being delayed probably by sabotage and certainly by lack of materials. The Germans had other priorities and, as the sea war swung in the Allies' favour, there was less and less opportunity to employ an ocean-going ship as either a raider or a blockade runner. On completion in 12th January 1944 the ship was delivered as Wolta. Initially she was managed by the Deutsche Afrika Linien of Hamburg and served as target and accommodation ship for the 27th U-boat flotilla. Presumably this was regarded as playing a valuable part in Germany's war effort. Continuing in a sedentary role, she later became an accommodation ship for the Luftwaffe and in May 1945 was recovered by the Allies in the port of Flensburg.

On her return to Rotterdam she was not allowed to enter her owner's service immediately. Instead, on 21st November 1945, she sailed for New York and Surabaya carrying general cargo on behalf of the Dutch Government. On her return voyage from Indonesia she was on charter to the Vereenigde Nederlandse Scheepvaart Maatschappij for their Holland-Australia Line. Only on 26th July 1946 did Aldabi enter her intended trade, the Rotterdam Zuid Amerika Lijn service.

During her years with the Rotterdam South America Line Aldabi sailed a total of 1,115,000 million nautical miles and carried 895,000 tonnes of cargo. The only untoward incident occurred in 1956. While discharging her cargo in the Lekhaven in Rotterdam, the Aldabi's port side was extensively damaged by the Liberian-flag Melody, which had lost steerage way and rammed the Dutch ship. After discharging some 5,000 tonnes of wheat and frozen meat destined for Hamburg and Bremen, the Aldabi went into dry dock for repairs.

On 11th May 1967 Aldabi was sold and handed over in the Waalhaven, Rotterdam to the Alda Shipping Co. of Cyprus who simply shortened her name to Alda. Transfer in 1969 to Astrodesco Compania Naviera, Piraeus,

Greece was not accompanied by renaming. On 17th September 1971 Alda was laid up near Chalkis in Greece and in the spring of 1972 she was sold for scrap. She arrived in Istanbul on 9th May 1972 for demolition at Metan Agir Celik Izabe Sanayi.

Van Nievelt Goudriaan & Co's Stoomvaartmaatschappij had its origins in 1905, when two young men from Rotterdam's shipping community got together, H.A. van Nievelt and A.J.M. Goudriaan. Initially they owned modest-sized tramps, ideal for working in the Baltic timber trade. Their ships were generally named after stars, latterly with names beginning with Al, reflecting the names given by the Arab astronomers who discovered and named many heavenly bodies.

The company prospered greatly during the First World War, as did other shipping companies in neutral Holland, and more and bigger ships joined the fleet. The larger ships were either chartered to Dutch cargo liner companies, or put on the company's own service, the Rotterdam Zuid Amerika Lijn, founded in 1920. During the 1930s, black hulls gave way to grey, although ships on charter were often painted in the charterer's colours.

Despite losses during the Second World War, the company showed a renewed dynamism in early post-war years. Alongside its ocean cargo ships, it built some small motor coasters, in which the Dutch successfully specialised. A number of oil tankers were owned or managed, and a fleet of 14 fruit ships were operated on behalf of the US-based banana giant, United Fruit. Perhaps the most unusual assignment was management of two Dutch weather ships which were stationed in the North Atlantic, Cirrus and Cumulus.

Sadly, this diversification did not save the company, and in 1991 it applied to a Rotterdam court for protection against its creditors, and within a year this once considerable ship owner's fleet was dispersed.

Completed in 1940 by the Nederlandsche Dok Maaatschappij N.V., Amsterdam.
7,239 gross tons, 451 feet.
Machinery: eight-cylinder oil engine by Gebroeder Stork & Co. N.V., Hengelo.

Aldabi.

Aldabi at sea

ROYAL IRIS

1932–1950

Wallasey Corporation, Wallasey

The compilers need no excuse to include a Mersey ferry in this book, as most of their early memories of ships come from this river, where the ferries were (and remain) an important part of the shipping scene. When ships were routinely anchored in the Sloyne to await a berth, the ferry provided a superb vantage point. And the floating landing stages on both sides of the river had an atmosphere of their own. On the Wirral side, where the writer began his ship watching trips in the 1950s, walking down the covered way that connected the land and stage was an exciting experience of emerging into a different world of river light, salt air, wind-whipped muddy water, and – if one was lucky – a panorama of ships.

There are at least ten ferry crossings of the Mersey known, almost invariably terminating at the point now known as the Pier Head in Liverpool. The three northernmost ferries, to New Brighton, Egerton and Seacombe, were amongst the last to be opened as urbanisation spread north along the Wirral Peninsula. The newly-created borough of Wallasey took these three ferries into municipal ownership in 1861, a move towards integrated transport as it would later direct its buses to serve its ferry terminals.

Wallasey considered itself somewhat superior to other boroughs, particularly its neighbour Birkenhead, and it did indeed have some upmarket areas. But in addition to middle-class commuters heading to the shipping and insurance offices in downtown Liverpool, it had another type of customer. As its name suggests, New Brighton was developed as a seaside resort and attracted vast numbers of day trippers from Liverpool and the industrial areas of the Wirral. On high days and holidays Wallasey ferries had to cater for these as well as the borough's more affluent residents, and hence its ferries had massive capacities. *Royal Iris* was certificated for 2,024, at least as many as any of the big Atlantic liners depicted elsewhere in this book, although of course there were no berths for all these passengers, and probably not even enough seats.

Their massive capacity, shallow draft and numerous water-tight compartments made Wallasey ferries particularly attractive to the Admiralty during the First World War, and this led to the *Royal Iris* acquiring the prefix to her

name. Her predecessor ferries, *Iris* and *Daffodil*, were requisitioned early in 1918, and on St George's Day played a prominent role in the attack on the German naval base at Zeebrugge in occupied Belgium. In what would later be called a commando raid, the *Iris* and *Daffodil* transferred troops from bigger ships to the mole, their shallow draft enabling them to get in close. Although the operation had limited military success and there were heavy casualties, the *Iris* and *Daffodil* were feted on their return to the Mersey in May, being put on display with their battle damage for all to see. At the suggestion of Wallasey Corporation, King George V allowed the ferries to be renamed *Royal Iris* and *Royal Daffodil*, and this privilege was to be enjoyed by their successors. However, the Corporation's incompetence in not ensuring that her name was reserved when the original *Royal Iris* was sold in 1931 meant her successor, depicted in the painting, had to make do with the name *Royal Iris II* until 1947. In fact, she carried the name *Royal Iris* only until 1950 when the imminent launch of a successor required her to be renamed *St. Hilary*. She was sold to Holland in 1956 and underwent a rather dramatic conversion to a car ferry.

The third *Royal Iris* launched in 1950 could not have been more different: a radical attempt to design a vessel for both ferry work and cruising, which some unkind commentators felt had been created by someone more familiar with building buses. Her catering arrangements led her to be dubbed the 'floating fish and chip shop'. After she in turn was sold in 1993, an existing Birkenhead ferry was chosen to keep the traditional title alive, although it became the cumbersome *Royal Iris of the Mersey*. Their heyday is long past but, the ferries have achieved such iconic status that they are likely to continue their well subsidised river crossings and cruises for some years.

The *Royal Iris* of 1950.

Built in 1932 by Harland and Wolff Ltd., Govan.
607 gross tons, 151 feet.
Machinery: six-cylinder triple expansion engine by D. and W. Henderson and Co. Ltd., Glasgow, driving twin shafts.

Royal Iris approaches Prince's Landing Stage, Liverpool

OSCAR II
1909–1910
Haakon J. Wallem, Hong Kong

Norwegians have often been highly successful in the shipping business despite their country's lack of industry and trade. This story brings together the Norwegian owners of the world's largest ship and a group founded almost 100 years earlier by a fellow countryman and which has recently achieved major prominence in ship management.

Haakon Wallem was born in Bergen in 1870, and quickly left home to gain experience in shipping offices in London and Hamburg, before going out to Vladivostok and later Shanghai, where many foreign powers had concessions that were virtually autonomous areas of the city. During 1898 Wallem set himself up in the Chinese city as a chartering broker, and gradually moved into shipowning on his own account.

These were tumultuous but exciting times to be in China. Resentment of the power of foreigners in the country bubbled over into the Boxer Rebellion in 1900, and the deaths of some 200 westerners in Peking led to a multi-national force being put together to end the rebellion. The result was even more concessions to western governments, and the eventual overthrow of the ruling dynasty in 1911. Despite these events, Shanghai and its foreigners prospered and the city became the commercial capital of China. Wallem and others benefited from the Russo-Japanese War of 1904-5, which saw freight rates soar.

Oscar II was a significant ship for Wallem, his fourth and the biggest bought so far, but she was unfortunate in being lost less than a year after being acquired from Jacob Christensen of Bergen in 1909. On 22nd January 1910 *Oscar II* had just left Singapore on a voyage to Hamburg with rice when she went ashore on Bintan Island. Although refloated and returned to Singapore, she was thereafter fit only for use as a hulk.

Just before the First World War, Wallem took his young family back to Bergen, but his shipowning ventures there left him impecunious and embittered thanks to the slump which followed the ending of the war. He therefore returned to Shanghai and began again, building up a fleet which was officered

by Norwegians and crewed by Chinese. Good contacts, especially with the Hong Kong and Shanghai Bank, helped him greatly. For instance, ships of small Chinese owners who would not be seen as creditworthy by financial institutions were registered under Wallem's name: perhaps the most notable of these was C.Y. Tung.

The Wallem Group's spectacular growth has come since 1971, when the company moved into ship management. With shipowners in high-cost European countries looking to subcontract management and crewing, Wallem rapidly built up a large business, with at any one time some 130 ships fully managed and another 50 crewed from their Hong Kong office.

Amongst the managed ships has been the world's largest ship, the *Jahre Viking*. Her history is chequered, as her original owners went bankrupt whilst she was building. C.Y. Tung was offered the uncompleted vessel, but imposed an unusual condition, that the hull be significantly lengthened to make her the largest ship in the world, and this resulted in a gross tonnage of 565,000. *Seawise Giant*, as she was completed in 1981, spent only two years trading between the Middle East and Japan before being relegated to use as a storage hulk at an Iranian port. In May 1988 she was seriously damaged by a missile attack at the height of the Iran-Iraq war. Although a constructive total loss, the hulk was bought by Norwegian investors and towed to Singapore for a massive refit. In 1991 she emerged as seen in the inset painting as *Jahre Viking* under the Norwegian flag and Wallem management, the latter only ending in 2004 when she once more reverted to the role of a storage hull in the Arabian Gulf.

The two very different ships depicted here are symbols of how the enterprise of shipowners from a small country has helped shape the world's shipping industry.

Oscar II
Completed in 1893 by William Gray and Co. Ltd., Hartlepool.
3,060 gross tons, 317 feet.
Machinery: triple-expansion engine by Central Marine Engine Works, Hartlepool.

Jahre Viking, the world's largest ship.

Oscar II at Hong Kong

WIMBLEDON
1958–1967
Britain Steamship Co. Ltd. (Watts, Watts and Co. Ltd., managers), London

The title 'tramp' hardly applies to an innovative and well appointed ship like *Wimbledon*, and although tramping was her owner's basic trade, the ship spent most of her career as a cargo liner. From 1960 to 1965, for instance, she ran in Port Line colours as *Port Wimbledon*.

Watts, Watts had an enviable record for designing ships that were not only effective cargo carriers but also set new standards in crew accommodation. Their managing director Edmund Watts read a paper on the subject of crew accommodation in tramp ships to the Institution of Naval Architects in April 1949. He began by painting a picture of conditions in the 1920s. The ratings lived in the forecastle, sleeping in double-tiered bunks, and eating where they slept. Whereas it was not far to carry the captain's and navigating officers' food from galley to saloon, a 30 foot walk was usually needed, mostly in the open, to get it to the engineer's mess. And the walk from galley to forecastle was, he maintained, long enough to ruin any food. He was not impressed with the usual positioning of the galley at the fore end of the engine room casing where the ship took most water.

Watts then contrasted conditions in his own company's recent ships. In their new *Wanstead*, all accommodation was amidships, the majority being in the 'tween decks and trunked around numbers 3 and 4 hatches. A single cabin was provided for most members of the crew. There were no outside cabins, the accommodation in the 'tween decks being so arranged that recreational galleries occupied both port and starboard sides, with cabins opening inboard from these. The crew had a cafeteria (one of the first in a British ship) in the 'tween decks, whilst the officers had their dining room a deck higher: separate provisions which now seem wasteful but which were considered essential in the late 1940s. The design of the *Wimbledon* and her sisters, *Weybridge* and *Willesden*, continued the principle of situating the single-berth cabins inboard of long galleries at either side of the ship. The high waist which the class were given, and moving their engines much further aft, gave the new class a very different, and indeed unique, profile.

A distinctive feature was the prominent knuckle in the hull at bow and stern, which had a beneficial effect on heavy weather behaviour by increasing buoyancy, and this is credited to Edmund Watts. Specially designed fins were fitted by the propellor to give a better flow of water, increasing manoeuvrability and adding half a knot to the ship's speed. One of the features the technical press got excited about was the gas turbine generator, for use when the main engines were not running. The hot exhaust gases from this unit supplied most of the ship's heating requirements. The journalist from the 'The Motor Ship' who attended the trials of the first of the class was impressed by how quickly the generator could be put on load, and by its relative quietness.

It is probably no coincidence that Watts, Watt's *Wimbledon*, along with her predecessor *Wanstead* of 1949, was chartered by Port Line: their respective founders, Edmund Watts and William Milburn, were once partners. When they went their separate ways in 1879, Watts concentrated on tramp trades. He later moved to London and named his ships after suburbs of the capital or towns in the south east; latterly all with names beginning with the letter W.

Wimbledon only carried this name for a total of four years, from completion in 1958 to 1960, and from 1965 to 1967 when she was sold. New owners were Pakistan's National Shipping Corporation, who were building up their fleet following pressure from their government for Pakistan's ships to gain a share of the trade to their country. Her new name was *Swat*, as which she often reappeared in British ports. She was broken up at Karachi in late 1982.

The relatively early sales of *Wimbledon* and her sisters probably reflected the diminishing interest of the Watts family in shipping after Edward Watts died in 1962, and in 1968 the shipowning company, Britain Steamship Co. Ltd., was sold to Bibby. It marked the end of one of the UK's longest-lived and most innovative tramp fleets.

Completed in 1958 by Barclay, Curle and Co. Ltd., Glasgow.
9,223 gross tons, 488 feet overall.
Machinery: Doxford-type six-cylinder oil engine by Barclay, Curle and Co. Ltd., Glasgow

Port Wimbledon. [Ian Farquhar]

Wimbledon leaves Barclay, Curle's yard in 1958

DEPARTURE AND ARRIVAL – 1

I was first appointed to the *Canberra* as a junior fourth officer – a rank that no longer exists – in January 1968. I had just completed my apprenticeship and had a brand new second mate's ticket, on which the ink was barely dry. This was the time of white number 10 day uniforms, often referred to as 'ice cream suits', which were so heavily starched by the laundry that you could often tear a trouser leg off whilst trying to force a foot through. Sitting down in this uniform was virtually out of the question.

The Captain at the time was of vast proportions and a fearsome man, who had little time for junior ranks and I tried my best to keep clear of him. I did by chance bump into him one morning and somewhat breezily and nervously said 'Good morning sir'. His reply rumbled down from on high, and was 'When I want a weather report I will ask'. I had little further contact with him for the year I was on board.

I returned to *Canberra* for six weeks as First Officer in 1979, when I first met my future wife Angela Thomas who was employed as an entertainments officer. I had further periods onboard as Deputy Captain 1990 and 1991 to 1993. In 1997 I was appointed her Captain; I hope a friendlier one than the first I encountered, and that was how I found myself in charge on 10th October 1997 on her final voyage to the graveyard at Gadani Beach, situated a short distance north of Karachi.

We sailed on this voyage from Southampton at 21.00, with a ship's company of 72, including one lady Purser Officer, the wife of our Chief Officer/Staff Captain/Doctor Phil Bowler. The Chief Engineer was the specially promoted and vastly *Canberra*-experienced David Barraclough, Chief Electrician Alex Jamison, Chief Radio Officer Freddie Lloyd and two chefs - David Mclachlan and Greg Harris. All were without doubt amongst some of the greatest characters I have met at sea. We departed to the skirl of bagpipes playing 'Flowers of the Forest', 'Lonely Night at the Bothy' and 'Dark Isle', which to say the least was an emotional experience. We were subject to a water jet display as we passed Fawley Oil Refinery and were greeted by the ferry *Pride of Bilbao* as we exited the Solent via the Nab Tower into the English Channel: the ferry's Captain, Bob Ross, had served on *Canberra*.

The ship looked immaculate both inside and out and I moved all the crew into passenger cabins so that everyone had a phone. Many who were used to sharing a cabin found themselves ensconced in a suite. We made the Bonito Club, a beautiful room that had once been the first class ballroom, into the wardroom and general meeting area for all onboard, and although dress during the day was somewhat casual compared with our normal standards, we all wore Red Sea Rig in the evenings from 18.00, which was again a novel experience for many. The ship had been left well stocked with everything we could need and indeed a lot more, and we ate extremely well in the Pacific Restaurant. The two chefs excelled themselves with extensive menus of mouth watering delights being produced every day, and it was not long before we were all showing the effects of this. Luckily the slops locker had also been left well stocked and we were able to move into new uniforms as our changing shapes dictated. The ship's laundry was operational and a full service was offered. We removed the long stainless steel laundry trough to the Bonito Pool area and made it into a slide from the deck above to the pool.

We soon settled into a relaxed and enjoyable routine as we enjoyed an 8½ day cruise to Port Said where we dropped anchor at the Charlie 5 Anchorage at 09.45 on 19th October. It was virtually an incident-free passage and the only thing I can recall was that the 'Ship Captain's Medical Guide' – the medical Bible – went missing but was soon anonymously returned following a somewhat stern tannoy message from myself. Possibly the quick return was because of the graphic pictures contained within the tome, especially the ones of what are known as social diseases. At Port Said we took on a passenger in the form of a goat that was destined to make

the ultimate sacrifice for our Pakistani general purpose crew who are particularly fond of its meat. At 21.47 we weighed anchor and transited the Suez Canal on the most beautiful of starlight nights; it was a wonderful experience and a shame that passengers could not share in it.

Having cleared the Canal we anchored at 10.30 on 20th October in Suez Bay just outside port limits to avoid dues, where we bunkered fuel. At 18.26 we weighed anchor and departed celebrating with an excellent goat curry for dinner. On 22nd I received a message from our office stating that the Memorandum of Agreement (the sale document) had been signed and that our final destination was to be Gadani Beach; up to this time we had not been definitely confirmed.

During our passage to Karachi we enjoyed the calmest 7½ days at sea that I have ever experienced. Again there were no incidents, although I remember the excitement of the capture of a wild hawk that had made the ship its home, the robin that got into my night cabin and had tried to nest on my chest whilst I was asleep (I don't know who was more outraged when I woke up) and the feverish activity of the various departments as they built their boats for the Bonito Pool regatta. This event was staged on Sunday 26th with much enthusiasm and excitement, and I have to admit that the deck department's entry capsized on being launched into the pool. We anchored about 12 miles off Karachi (again to avoid dues) at 07.21 on 28th October. With my limited use of Urdu I had difficulty in explaining to port control over the VHF radio as to why we had called, and eventually made all the arrangements through the bridge seaman. Our agents arrived at 15.25, and at 09.25 the following morning the soon-to-be-owner boarded. I walked him round the ship which looked magnificent and he kept asking me why were we selling her! At 12.00 the Physical Delivery Certificate was signed and at 15.00 the new owner and his entourage went ashore, leaving us wondering what was happening. There had been discussion about the ship's company leaving the ship prior to departure for Gadani, but the Beaching Master had taken one look at the bridge and the engine room and requested that the entire complement remain for the beaching operation. This I know pleased everyone as *Canberra* was held in great affection and pride and everyone wanted to see the job through to completion as a team.

At 19.00 on 30th October the beaching crew boarded and at 20.34 with the anchor aweigh we set off on the last leg of our journey. At 23.06 we anchored off Gadani Beach for the night awaiting the correct tidal conditions in the morning. At 08.39 on 31st October the anchor was aweigh for the last time and the ship with a trim to match the slope angle of the beach was taken about eight miles out to sea, turned and run in at just over 20 knots (90 rpm) for the beach. None of us knew what to expect and we all not surprisingly hung on to what ever was nearest. In the event we beached 2,100 feet from the water's edge with the full length of the ship at 09.40 at a draft of 28' 8'' forward and 34' 4'' aft, at what is known as Plot 54/55 Gadani Beach. We never even felt a shudder as we came to a halt, cracked a good bottle of iced champagne on the bridge – contrary to company regulations – and shut the ship down. As we grounded I couldn't resist repeating the well known football phrase – 'There are people on the beach. They think it's all over. It is now'.

At 13.00 we disembarked using our own tenders and ran the boats onto the beach, here we jumped out and manhandled our baggage ashore rather like shipwrecked sailors. Our agent was on hand and we were taken to our hotels in Karachi before flying home. Although it was a sad event seeing the demise of a famous ship it was also a wonderfully unique and unforgettable experience. I am proud to have been part of this ship's company where during this voyage we became a close knit and efficient unit facing all sorts of unusual challenges, and most importantly we all had an enjoyable time and have great memories.

Captain Mike Carr

Canberra arrives at the breakers

DEPARTURE AND ARRIVAL – 2

The first time I saw *Queen Elizabeth 2* was on a grim, rainy morning in Southampton. I was standing on the bridge of *Canberra*, looking south through a pair of binoculars. A deck cadet, just finishing my training, I was elated by the distant scene as she turned off her berth. My excitement was evidently not shared by the other officers on *Canberra's* bridge as Cunard was after all the long-time nemesis of P&O. Both companies in existence since the 1840s, they had been establishing their own heritage independently but parallel for well over a century. I was intimately aware of P&O's traditions and history but somehow the sighting of the iconic *Queen Elizabeth 2* left me wondering about what seemed a greater heritage of the transatlantic liner company. Needless to say, I did not let my blasphemous thoughts be known to those around me. Little did I know then that a decade later I would find myself on the bridge of *Queen Elizabeth 2* as a deck officer, once again smiling below my binoculars, but this time looking north along Southampton's famous waterfront at my earlier posting, the 'Great White Whale' herself, *Canberra*.

I was extremely lucky to have served on both ships. They left indelible marks on my life with their very different appearances and abilities both inside and out, aesthetically and technically. However, they did have something in common; they both had a soul. That very tangible but ethereal, almost sentient, existence that makes some ships feel alive. I'm sure that any deck officer or ship master will agree with me when they recall standing at the conn of their charge whilst endeavouring to perform a challenging manoeuvre into a berth or during a heavy storm during the dead of night. They will surely admit to quietly talking to the ship under their breath. (At these times the ship is most definitely female, incidentally). This almost intimate communication with the ship under times of quiet concentration is far more prevalent in ships with a soul, in ships that their master's feel an empathy toward. This was definitely the case with *Canberra* and *Queen Elizabeth 2*.

The departure of *Canberra* to the breakers' yard at Gadani Beach, so magnificently but sadly portrayed by Robert in this book, brought not only a lump to my throat for the final departure of that ship's soul but also fresh fuel to the argument that the ocean liner's days were numbered and that *Queen Elizabeth 2* would be the last. She was, after all, not only the one remaining ocean liner to be plying her trade on the Atlantic but anywhere on the globe. The two sides of the argument became increasingly unbalanced as it became more and more certain in today's cut-throat and fiscally fit business world that the building of a new ocean liner would not be viable, that the return against investment for the shareholders is much more gratifying in the building of the ubiquitous cruise ship.

My brain told me to agree with this argument but my heart appealed to me to be

less hasty. The argument shifted back toward the possible continuation of the ocean liner upon Carnival Corporation's acquisition of Cunard Line in 1998. Now at least the company had a ship owner in charge and prospects were looking good. A few years after my days on *Queen Elizabeth 2*'s bridge I found myself shoreside in Cunard's headquarters being appointed to represent the company in the planning, design, construction, outfitting and delivery of *Queen Mary 2*. My heart's side of the argument had won. *Queen Mary 2* had been ordered for Cunard by Carnival. The next great ocean liner was finally on her way.

As Cunard's Director of New Builds, the planning, design, testing, retesting, construction and outfitting was all-encompassing for me in the five years leading up to her delivery. It became apparent from the very beginning that she too had a strong soul. She had an inherently good feeling about her at all times, even during the dead of night when few workers were around and the ship was largely in darkness. Every one of the countless number of times I travelled to northern France from Miami and saw her built just a little bit more with another block proudly in place, I could swear that it was almost as if she were patiently waiting, benevolently allowing the thousands of workers to clamber about her as she grew. That is right up until the latter stages when she seemed keen to get to sea like a pedigree horse at the starting gate.

We faced many challenges along the way but each time we tested and perhaps changed a piece of machinery the ship would almost encourage us in her silent but seemingly living presence. Whenever we had a test of some critical piece of equipment or procedure, she inevitably passed with consummate ease. Appreciate now that there was an incredible amount of ground-breaking technology and techniques involved. She breezed through them all. The ocean liner was back. Delivered on time, complete and below budget, her introduction to the world was nothing short of incredible. Hundreds of thousand turned out to welcome her around the world as well as heads of state and countless celebrities.

The meeting in Southampton with her younger sibling *Queen Elizabeth 2* marked a symbolic handing over of the baton. *Queen Elizabeth 2* could now relax. She no longer had to support the mantle of being the last true ocean liner. Her heritage, traditions and knowledge of 165 years could be passed to *Queen Mary 2*.

The irony that this handing over occurred in Southampton, so beautifully portrayed here by Robert, is not lost on me. It represents a very happy and complete circle in my life. I feel very content knowing that the ocean liner is not gone and that *Queen Mary 2* has shown that the ocean liner's existence is perfectly viable in today's industry. And I think she knows it.

Gerry Ellis

Queen Mary 2 meets *Queen Elizabeth 2* at Southampton

Acknowledgements

I would like to thank all those who have generously given their time and experience in the creation of this book. Firstly, my grateful thanks to Efthimios E. Mitropoulos, Secretary-General of the International Maritime Organization for writing the introduction for this book. His words perfectly sum up not only the importance of shipping in world economic terms but also the 'feeling' of a ship at sea or in dock; whether a classic liner or modern supertanker, each has an undeniable 'presence' which is the one thing that drew me to paint them in the first place

Thanks to Gerry Ellis at Carnival Corporation for his wonderful summary not only of the *Queen Mary 2* but also the genuine viability of liners in general. My thanks also to all those customers and friends from around the world for their generous support and for their contributions, including Rob Grool at Wallem Ship Management, David Kenwright at Gulf Offshore, Karl-Heinz Hilbig at Triton and Seatrade Groningen, and Chi Chien Hsu at Eddie Steamship Co. My thanks also to all those who have not only contributed their knowledge and expertise but also allowed their paintings to reproduced here: Tom Cassidy, Stephen Payne, Commodore Ron and Kim Warwick, Gary Davies, Richard Clack, Ian Howatson, Robert Hunter, Richard Faber, Miles Cowsill, Paul Jacobs and his team at Wisteria Gallery for the perfect frame, Colin Fanning for his photographic expertise, Des and Ulla Cox for their unwavering support and friendship, George O'Hara, Paul Wood, Terry Connell, Kevin Wells, Glen Smith, Michael French, Michael Whitingham, Barry Rubery for continued support, and of course all those who have allowed their paintings to be included and have contributed their memories and technical expertise.

Special thanks to Roy Fenton in his capacity as writer and editor and of course to him and John Clarkson at Ships in Focus for their 'nerve' to commit to not one, but two books!

Lastly and perhaps most importantly to my wife Vicky for her continuous help and encouragement and for her support of the often temperamental 'artist'. This book is dedicated to Vicky and my daughter Emilia whose little fingerprints always seem to appear from nowhere!

Robert Lloyd

Sources

BANK LINE LTD.
Appleyard HS. *Bank Line 1885-1985* World Ship Society, Kendal, 1985
Boot P. 'Themes and variations: the development of post-war Bank Line cargo ships' *Ships in Focus Record* Nos 17, 2001, pages 50-59 and 18, 2001, pages 112-121
BEN LINE STEAMERS LTD.
Somner G. *Ben Line: Fleet List and Short History* World Ship Society, Kendal, 1980
BIBBY LINE LTD.
Watson W. *The Bibby Line 1807-1990* James and

James, London, 1990
Haws D. *Merchant Fleets 29: The Burma Boats, Bibby and Henderson* TCL Publications, Uckfield, 1995
BLUE FUNNEL LINE
Clarkson J, Harvey W, Fenton R. *Ships in Focus: Blue Funnel Line.* Ships in Focus Publications, Preston, 1998
Marshall M. *There Go the Ships.* Memoir Club, Spennymoor, 2003
Bell MD. 'Gorgon – memories of a Blue Funnel Liner.' *Ships Monthly*, 22, March 1987.
BLUE STAR LINE LTD.
Atkinson T, O'Donoghue K. *Blue Star.* Kendal, World Ship Society, 1985
Kinghorn AW. 'The Two Dunedin Stars'. *Ships in Focus Record* No 9, 1999, pages 17-21
Kinghorn AW. 'The Welly Boot'. *Ships in Focus Record* No 17, 2001, pages 34-41
The text for *Brasilia Star* has been adapted, with the author's kind permission, from Kinghorn AW. 'Queensland-Brasilia Star' *Ships in Focus Record* No 23, 184-188
Part of the text for *Auckland Star* has been taken, again with the author's permission, from Kinghorn AW *Before the Box Boats* Kenneth Mason, Emsworth, 1983
BOWATER STEAMSHIP CO. LTD.
'Fleet in Focus: Bowaters' *Ships in Focus Record* No 5, 1998, pages 3-16
B.P. TANKER CO. LTD.
Thanks to David Kenwright and Murray G. Smith.
BRITISH INDIA STEAM NAVIGATION CO. LTD.
Laxon WA and Perry FW *BI: The British India Steam Navigation Co. Ltd.* World Ship Society, Kendal, 1994
CANADIAN PACIFIC STEAMSHIPS LTD.
Musk G. *Canadian Pacific Afloat 1883-1968. A Short History and Fleet List.* Canadian Pacific, London, 1968
Haws D, *Merchant Fleets 23: Canadian Pacific* TCL Publications, Hereford, 1991.
Thanks to Bill Cunningham of Carterton, New Zealand.
CHINA NAVIGATION CO. LTD.
Haws D. *Merchant Fleets 39: China Navigation Company*, TCL Publications, Pembroke, 2001
Dick HW and Kentwell SA. *Beancaker to Boxboat: Steamship Companies in Chinese Waters*, Nautical Association of Australia Inc, Canberra, 1988
Thanks to T H Connell.
CUNARD STEAMSHIP CO. LTD.
Blair C. *Hitler's U-boat War: the Hunted 1942-1945* Weidenfeld and Nicholson, London, 1999
Buxton I. *Metal Industries: Shipbreaking at Rosyth and Charlestown* World Ship Society, Kendal, 1992
Clarke JF. *Building Ships on the North East Coast: Part 1 c 1640-1914* Bewick Press, Whitley Bay, 1997
Dodman FE. *Ships of the Cunard Line* Adlard Coles, Southampton, 1955
Haws D. *Merchant Fleets 19: White Star Line* Travel Creatours Ltd., Hereford, 1991
Haws D. *Triumph of a Great Tradition.* Cunard, London, 1990
Isherwood JH. *Cunard Portraits* World Ship Society, Kendal, 1990
Kludas A. *Great Passenger Ships of the World:*

Volume 1 1858-1912. Patrick Stephens, Cambridge, 1975
Le Fleming HM. *Cunard White Star Liners of the 1930s.* Ian Allan, London, 1960
Streater L. *Berengaria: Cunard's 'Happy Ship'* Tempus, Stroud, 2001
Thanks to Alan Phipps.
EDDIE STEAMSHIP CO. LTD.
Thanks to Chih-Chien Hsu.
ELLERMAN AND BUCKNALL STEAMSHIP CO. LTD.
Taylor JA. *Ellermans: A Wealth of Shipping* Wilton House, London
Haws D. *Merchant Fleets 16: Ellerman Lines* TCL Publications, Hereford, 1989
Clarkson J and Fenton R. *Ships in Focus: Ellerman Lines* Ships in Focus, Preston, 1993
Thanks to Captain D.M. Bridge.
FEDERAL STEAM NAVIGATION CO. LTD.
Clarkson J, Fenton R. *Ships in Focus: New Zealand and Federal Lines.* Ships in Focus, Preston, 1995
Thanks to Captain Glen Smith.
HAPAG-LLOYD A.G.
Isherwood JH. 'Steamers of the Past: Sud Atlantique Liner Pasteur of 1939' *Sea Breezes*, LVIII, 1984, pages 242-247
Thanks also to Karl-Heinz Hilbig.
T. AND J. HARRISON LTD.
Thanks to Graeme Cubbin and George Nicholson
G. HEYN AND SONS LTD
Harvey WJ. *Head Line: G. Heyn and Sons Ltd.* World Ship Society, Kendal, 1990
The account of Captain Black's career is adapted from this book, with the author's permission.
HOLLAND-AMERIKA LIJN
Payne S. 'The Darling of the Dutch' *Ships Monthly*, 30, August and September 1995.
ISLE OF MAN STEAM PACKET CO. LTD.
Henry, F. *Ships of the Isle of Man Steam Packet Company Limited.* Brown, Son and Ferguson, Glasgow, 1967
Chappell, C. *Island Lifeline* T. Stephenson, Prescot, 1980
'ITALIA' SOCIETA PER AZIONI DI NAVIGAZIONE
Hocking C. *Dictionary of Disasters at Sea during the Age of Steam* Lloyd's Register of Shipping, London, 1969
Thanks to Richard Faber
LAMPORT AND HOLT LINE LTD.
Hackman R. 'Lamport and Holt's Vs'. *Ships in Focus Record* No. 15, 2001, 144-153
LYKES BROTHERS STEAMSHIP CO. INC.
Sawyer LA and Mitchell WH. *From America to United States, Part Two.* WSS, Kendal, 1981
NEW ZEALAND SHIPPING CO. LTD.
Clarkson J, Fenton R. *Ships in Focus: New Zealand and Federal Lines.* Ships in Focus, Preston, 1995
Watson W. 'An Engineer's Voyage Down Under' *Ships Monthly*, 37, March 2002
Thanks also to W.H Watson for further memories.
ORIENT STEAM NAVIGATION CO. LTD., LONDON
Newall P. *Orient Line* Ships in Focus, Preston, 2004
Thanks to Commodore Ian Gibb and Captain J.L. Chapman.

NIPPON YUSEN KAISHA
Thanks to Alan Watt.
P&O STEAM NAVIGATION COMPANY
Rabson S, O'Donoghue K. *P&O: A Fleet History* World Ship Society, Kendal, 1988
PORT LINE LTD.
Newall P. 'Port Line's Golden Era' *Ships in Focus Record* No 13, 2000, pages 26-29 Spong HC. *Port Line* World Ship Society, Windsor, 2004
Thanks to John Burtt.
HILMAR REKSTEN
Pein JW. *Giganten der Weltmeere: die Geschicte der Supertanker* Koehler, Hamburg, 1976
ROYAL MAIL LINES LTD.
Haws D. *Merchant Fleets 5: Royal Mail Line and Nelson Line.* TCL Publications, Crowborough, 1982
Thanks also to Ralph Skinner and Bob Forrester of the Royal Mail Association, and to the contributors to the Association's excellent newsletter 'Royal Mail News', copies of which were kindly lent by Ralph.
SHAW, SAVILL AND ALBION CO. LTD.
De Kerbrech RP. *Shaw, Savill and Albion: the Post-war Fortunes of a Shipping Empire.* Conway Maritime, London, 1986
Mitchell A. *Splendid Sisters.* Harrap, London, 1966
Thanks to Edward Buckle and John Pitt-Stanley.
A/B SVENSKA AMERIKA LINIEN
McCart N. 'The Story of a Princess' *Ships Monthly*, 1991, 26
UNION-CASTLE MAIL STEAMSHIP CO. LTD.
Newall P. *Union-Castle Line: A Fleet History* Carmania Press, London, 1999
Hague A. 'Armed Merchant Cruisers' In Osborne R (ed) *Conversion for War* World Ship Society, Kendal, 1983
UNITED STATES LINES COMPANY
Fenton R. 'American Pioneers and Presidents' *Ships Monthly*, 2004, 39, 14-17
Kohler P. 'Blue Ribands and Record Breakers' *Ships Monthly*, 2004, 39, 26-29
Sawyer LA and Mitchell WH. *From America to United States, Part Two and Part Four.* WSS, Kendal, 1981 and 1986
Knego P. 'A visit to the United States' *Ships Monthly*, 1998, 33, 34-37
VAN NIEVELT GOUDRIAAN & CO.'S STOOMVAARTMAATS.
Haalmeijer F. *Van Nievelt Goudriaan & Co* Erato, Haarlem, 1980
WALLASEY CORPORATION
Maund TB and Jenkins M. *Mersey Ferries: Volume 2 – The Wallasey Ferries.* Black Dwarf Publications, Lydney, 2003
HAAKON WALLEM/WALLEM SHIPMANAGEMENT LTD.
Dick HW and Kentwell SA. *Sold East: Traders, Tramps and Tugs of Chinese Waters*, Nautical Association of Australia Inc, Melbourne, 1991
Hardy AJ. *Typhoon Wallem: a Personalised Chronicle of the Wallem Group Limited.* Granta Editions, Cambridge, 2003
WATTS, WATTS AND CO. LTD.
Fenton R. 'Wanstead to Woodford'. *Ships in Focus Record* No. 6, 1998 119-127
The Motor Ship, March 1958